Fifty Shades of Grace

Fifty Shades of Grace

Stories of Inspiration and Promise

Melodie M. Davis, Compiler

Foreword by Donald B. Kraybill

Herald Press

Harrisonburg, Virginia
Waterloo, Ontario

Libary of Congress Catalog-in-Publication Data
Fifty shades of grace : stories of inspiration and promise / Melodie
M. Davis, compiler.
    p. cm.
    ISBN 978-0-8361-9786-0 (pbk. : alk. paper) 1. Christian life. I.
Davis, Melodie M., 1951- editor of compilation.
    BV4515.3.F54 2013
    248.4—dc23
                                            2013006250

Unless otherwise noted, Scripture text is quoted, with permission,
from the *New Revised Standard Version*, © 1989, Division of
Christian Education of the National Council of Churches of Christ
in the United States of America. Scriptures quotations marked NIV
are from *New International Version*®, NIV® Copyright © 1973,
1978, 1984, 2011 by Biblica, Inc.™ Used by permission. All rights
reserved worldwide.

FIFTY SHADES OF GRACE:
STORIES OF INSPIRATION AND PROMISE
Copyright © 2013 by Herald Press, Harrisonburg, Virginia 22802
    Released simultaneously in Canada by Herald Press,
    Waterloo, Ontario N2L 6H7. All rights reserved.
Library of Congress Control Number: 2013006250
International Standard Book Number: 978-0-8361-9786-0
Printed in United States of America
Cover design by Merrill R. Miller, design by Joshua Byler
Cover photo by Leigh Prather/iStockphoto/Thinkstock

17 16 15 14 13   10 9 8 7 6 5 4 3 2 1

To order or request information, please call 1-800-245-7894 in the
U.S. or 1-800-631-6535 in Canada. Or visit www.heraldpress.com.

*To all who are aching for true love
and grace in their lives.*

Table of Contents

⁀

Pain

Reconciliation

Trust

Calling

Foreword

When Grace Walks in the Door

Donald B. Kraybill

∽

I confess. I had never really grappled with the notion of grace until October 2, 2006. Sure, I knew the words to "Amazing Grace" by memory. I knew grace was a gift from God, but I'd never seen it so vividly until the aftermath of the day Charlie walked into a one-room Amish school in Nickel Mines, Pennsylvania and shot ten young girls—killing five of them and inflicting the rest with life-threatening injuries. Charlie then took his own life at the scene.

Moments of compassion and forgiveness soon graced that horrific day as members of the Amish community reached out to Charlie's distraught family, who are not Amish. Seven hours after the shooting Charlie's mother saw an Amish neighbor whom she called "our Angel in black," walk in their front door. For over an hour, the neighbor kept repeating "we love you." The mother's pastor described it this way: "Grace walked through the door and with grace, came hope."

About the same time, a few miles away, grace walked through the door at the home of Charlie's widow and her parents as three Amish men arrived to offer words of love, forgiveness, and kindness. Grace also touched down at Charlie's burial when dozens of Amish people—including parents who had buried their own children a day or so before—hugged Charlie's widow and other family members. As surprised as everyone else, the funeral director noted in awe, "I witnessed a miracle today." Amish people also brought food and flowers to Charlie's home and contributed funds for his family. There were few words from Amish lips. It was mostly hugs, gifts, and presence—acts of grace— that communicated their forgiveness. The father of one of the slain girls explained, "Our forgiveness was not our words, it was what we did."

Perhaps you picked up this book because of the title. Over sixty-five million copies of a similar title, *Fifty Shades of Grey* have sold. The dark and troubled relationships of the *Fifty Shades* trilogy mirror the shards of brokenness in our lives and relationships. Surely, there must be more. Or at least we hope so.

Fifty Shades of Grace: Stories of Inspiration and Promise, offers a different take—a healing message for our sorrows and splintered relationships. These surprising stories unwrap the grace we sometimes discover in community and in our relationship with God. These vignettes offer good news in a world that glorifies "me" above "we" and too often leaves God out of the equation.

The writers of *Fifty Shades of Grace* share personal stories of goodness from all around the world. The stories compel, mesmerize, and strike again and again with wonderment for the many colors of God's lavish love. These contemporary stories of grace all rub against the grain of popular culture. They offer a redemptive counterpoint to the darkness and oppression lurking in the shadows of *Fifty Shades of Grey*. These storytellers open new doors through which we can recognize kindness and forgiveness from others and from God.

All of which takes me back to the Amish. After the shooting at Nickel Mines, I interviewed more than three dozen Amish people in preparation to coauthor *Amish Grace: How Forgiveness Transcended Tragedy.* I asked each person, "What motivated you to forgive?" Without exception they turned to the Lord's Prayer: "Forgive us *as* we forgive others." They also noted other New Testament Scriptures that underscore the stark adage: "Forgive and you will be forgiven." In the Anabaptist Christian tradition forgiveness has two dimensions. It is indeed a gift from God, but it expects that we will not hoard it, but indeed will pass it on to those who injure and harm us.

As a faith group, the Amish stay out of sync with popular culture, but in their separation from a world that applauds the right to revenge, the Amish have shown us a different shade of grace. Innumerable other unsung heroes of the Jesus way give quiet, daily witness to the power of forgiveness and the wonderment of grace. Such are the stories found in this book, many stemming from the same Anabaptist stream of faith birthed in the 1500s in the aftermath of the Protestant Reformation.

The paradox of grace is that it doesn't come in monocolor. Sometimes it drops in by surprise—an unexpected gift from God. Other times it arrives in the midst of sorrow and pain and still again it flutters into our lives in a time of joy. Sometimes the gift of grace is the fruit of seasoned preparation—a cultivated habit. Other times we find it in the midst of healing and reconciliation. Nevertheless one thing is clear: grace is not always cheap and easy but whenever it arrives, hope comes along as God's spirit visits the drab crevices and dry seasons of our lives.

—*Donald Kraybill, March 2013*

Donald B. Kraybill is author of the award-winning Upside-Down Kingdom *and coauthor of* Amish Grace: How Forgiveness Transcended Tragedy.

Introduction

∞

The idea for this book started with a somewhat raucous lunchroom brainstorming session at our MennoMedia office, taking off, of course, from the popularity of the *Fifty Shades of Grey* bestseller.

I didn't happen to be present, but I heard about the "Fifty Shades of Grace" idea immediately upon returning from a short vacation. What if we were to publish Christian stories of finding God's grace? Can something redeeming come out of an association with a trendy erotic romance novel?

You'll be able to judge for yourself in reading these simple but powerful stories from the lives of fifty ordinary people who have witnessed God's astounding and overflowing grace. Grace is something that Christians talk about a lot. It's the kind of unconditional love God demonstrated in Jesus' life, death, and resurrection. Even though we don't deserve God's love, it showers upon us anyway. We are forgiven, and God's Spirit enables us to offer grace to others.

The writers come from a variety of backgrounds. Theirs are stories of vocational change, grief and loss, divorce, long- or short-term mission work, ministry stories from pastors, teachers, parents, grandparents, ministries of the young and old.

It would be tempting to read all these engaging stories in one or two sessions, but I would suggest that you read them in daily or even weekly sessions over the course of a year. You will feel the impact again and again—in fresh ways with each new story. You will be alerted to experiences of grace that you might not otherwise recognize. A story that might not speak to you if you've read ten in a row may, over time, connect with your lived experiences. And hopefully you will grow to recognize opportunities to extend grace to another, or to see how someone has blessed you.

As one of the writers, Hannah Heinzekehr, puts it:

> Typically, when I think about grace, I think about times when I have failed or fallen short of deserving something and others have offered grace and forgiveness to me, even though I didn't deserve these gifts. Or, on the other hand, I can be the bringer of grace when I'm willing to pardon someone else who has wronged me. Sometimes in the Christian sphere, we use *grace* interchangeably with *salvation*. It's a gift that comes from God and through Jesus Christ to undeserving but penitent humans. It cannot be earned, but is bestowed despite our lack of merit.

May our stories inspire you to recall and learn from the amazing ways you too have seen and experienced God's grace.

—Melodie Davis, Compiler, February 2013

In a Flash

1

Grace Conductor

Janet Berg

∽

"**D**ad, Dad!" I shouted to the elderly man standing on the far end of the train platform, as I leaned out of the open train door. I knew I had only a few seconds to attract his attention before the train started moving again, and moments before I would be scolded by an Amtrak official. But I had promised my father that I would wave when we passed through Glasgow, Montana.

My husband and I were riding the train all the way from Chicago to Seattle, and we were relishing every minute of it. The scenery was breathtakingly beautiful—the first snow of the season had fallen during the night—and we were enjoying the enforced relaxation that comes with being in a place where there are virtually no decisions to be made.

But I had one tiny anxiety.

Weeks before, I had called my father, who lives in Glasgow, one of the small towns we would be traveling through on the train, and promised him I would wave. Now that we were on the train, the effort of getting out of my compartment even for a few minutes seemed huge. Besides, seeing anyone at a station was not going to be easy. But I hated to disappoint my ninety-year-old dad.

The train would stop in Glasgow only if passengers were getting on or off—and then only for a few moments. Even if we did stop, I would not be able to get off the train. All along our route, we were hearing stern announcements from the conductor that "we are now approaching" (and then he would name a town). "If this is not your stop, do *not* get off the train, or you may be left."

My dad had taken my promise to wave seriously, so we agreed that I would call him when the train left the stop before Glasgow, so he would know when to drive to the station. The train was running about an hour late by the time we reached Wolf Point, so I was not surprised that he answered immediately when I called. But I was astonished by what he said next. I was about to recommend that he not go to the station because of the snow, but he interrupted to say that he was already there, talking to some passengers waiting to board the train; he hoped to see me soon. Click. He hung up. That was it. He had perfect faith that he would see me.

What to do now? I knew that if I simply waved from the sleeper car we were in, Dad would never see me—my car could be a half-mile down the tracks by the time the train stopped. I decided I had to rouse myself from our cozy compartment and find the conductor, who had made all those stern announcements, to ask whether I could be at the one door that would open at the station. It took some doing, but I finally tracked him down and apologetically explained the situation. He looked at me for a moment over his glasses, then shuffled through his papers, talked with another official, and tersely said that they would be opening the third passenger car behind the dining car.

I immediately set out, walking through the train, careful to keep my balance as I walked through the dining car and then two passenger cars filled with people sleeping, talking, playing cards. I counted cars carefully and in the third one found my way down the narrow steps to the door. As I stood there alone, I started blaming myself because I hadn't taken my phone with me, and I hadn't told my husband where I was going. My mind whirled with a hundred questions: Should I walk back to the sleeper car to inform Al and get my phone? But what if I was walking back when we stopped in Glasgow and I missed Dad? Why is there no train official here to open the door? Aren't we almost there? Did I get the message right? What if they changed their minds and opened a different car?

After a few minutes, solitude and the mesmerizing sound of the train wheels had a calming effect. I was a kid again in Montana, the land of my childhood. Here there were many rules—like you should always honor your father and mother—but there was also lots of grace. Here people go out of their way to make things happen, just as my father was doing now, but when it doesn't work out, they don't spend much time blaming, as my father would not if he did not see me.

Finally the train slowed to a stop, and an employee came to open the door. I caught a glimpse of my dad, ninety years old, somewhat stooped but head up, eagerly scanning the windows for me. When all the passengers had boarded and Dad was the only person left on the platform, I stepped to the door and leaned out. "Dad!" I yelled to get his attention. He didn't hear me at first. "Dad, Dad!" I shouted again.

Then a most amazing thing happened. The conductor, who by now had miraculously appeared on the platform, joined me in the chorus of "Dad, Dad!" My father finally saw me and waved. I expected the train to start moving again, but it did not. The conductor made no move to reboard the train. Instead he addressed the lone man on the platform.

"Dad, come give your daughter a hug so we can get this train moving again" were his words. I was incredulous!

The Amtrak official was breaking his own rule! Without wasting a second to question him, I took that as my cue, hopped off the train, and ran toward my dad. With a big smile Dad hugged me, gave me a kiss, and told me he loved me.

My eyes were filled with tears. I do not know how I made it back into the train, but in a moment the door was shut and we were moving again. My Conductor of Grace was nowhere to be seen.

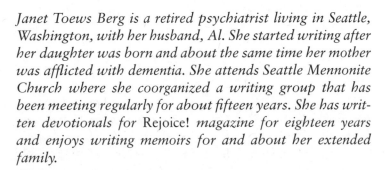

Janet Toews Berg is a retired psychiatrist living in Seattle, Washington, with her husband, Al. She started writing after her daughter was born and about the same time her mother was afflicted with dementia. She attends Seattle Mennonite Church where she coorganized a writing group that has been meeting regularly for about fifteen years. She has written devotionals for Rejoice! *magazine for eighteen years and enjoys writing memoirs for and about her extended family.*

2

A Moment of Clarity

Christopher Kennedy Lawford

∞

People ask me all the time why I was an addict. I tell them I think that I was a product of an addictive perfect storm. I have a genetic predisposition for addiction. In 1969, when I started down this road, it was a different time culturally. We were addicted to many, many things as a society. Our leaders talked about our addiction to oil.

Certain drugs were very much available. I was also a product of divorce and relocation at a very young age. I was the product of the trauma that I experienced when two of my uncles, President John F. Kennedy and Robert Kennedy were brutally assassinated in a very public way. It terrified me to death. At thirteen years old, I was looking for a way out.

My mom, God bless her, couldn't talk to me about drugs once she found out. She went out and tried to help with the "war on drugs," but right in our own house, I was falling apart. She couldn't talk to me because we didn't have *that* capacity. Many, many families don't have that capacity to really communicate.

Drugs and alcohol actually worked for my terrified feelings. If you're terrified or you're sad, that stuff works for a little while. If it didn't work, I wouldn't have done it. Problem is, it stops working, and for one in ten of us, even when it stops working, we keep doing it, because we have that predisposition for addiction.

My book *Moments of Clarity* came about because of my first book on this topic, *Symptoms of Withdrawal*. As I went out to talk about that book on addiction, people asked me, "What happened to you on February 17, 1986, that allowed you to change your life?"

First I say what happened to me was a moment of clarity, a moment of grace, a moment of profound transformation that I can only describe as God as I understand him, not God as a Catholic god or a Buddhist god or a Muslim god, but a God that's something inexplicable, out of this world. That thing came into my life because I had been beaten down to a point where I was open enough and surrendered enough to allow grace to pour into my life. That's what happened to me.

It has happened to a lot of people but it can be difficult to get people to talk about it. I've been able to get people like Anthony Hopkins, Richard Dreyfuss, Judy Collins, and more really amazing people to talk to me about their moments. Richard said to me, "Addicts and alcoholics are trying to find God. From the first moment, they're searching for a connection to God. And they use drugs and alcohol for that. And then they find it in recovery. That's their search." And I, on some level, believe that.

I tried for nine years to get sober. I tried everything. The great misperception is that addicts and alcoholics are shiftless and lazy, with no self-will. That's not the case. As a matter of fact, some of the most willful people I know are alcoholic and drug addicted. You try dancing with the eight hundred-pound gorilla of addiction while it's punching you in the face for nine years, and maintain any semblance of your life to keep going, and then tell me that someone with addiction doesn't have any willpower.

What does it mean to be addicted? My only purpose as an addict was to get the next thing I had to get to survive. That's the life of an addict. You don't think outside of that small linear box. Recovery, putting down the drugs and alcohol, doesn't mean you suddenly become a good person or a spiritual person. It means that you have a chance at that. An entire recovery involves thought, action, and spirit.

The process of recovery is a difficult one. You can't say, "Here, take this pill and you're fine." You can't say, "Go to this rehab once and you're fine." There is no trajectory of recovery. And that scares people. It's also terribly expensive.

The only thing you have to do right is not pick up a drink or drug a day at a time. But to change a human being is hard. Gandhi said the man who changes himself is greater than the man who conquers ten thousand armies. It is a very, very difficult thing to do, and many people can't do it. The core of all of this is that we're dealing with a disease, and this disease has a path like all diseases. Part of that path is relapse.

I come from a very willful and successful family. I come from a family where the ethic was that everyone can make a difference, and everyone should try. And what I found is the greatest gift in my life has been the ability to surrender, to give up. Because out of that comes unbelievable gifts, understanding, and compassion. Surrender is the greatest gift I've been given.

I'm so grateful that still, twenty-one years later [at the time of the interview; see bio], the best thing in the world is when another alcoholic reaches their hand out to me, that I can connect with another human being. As an alcoholic and an addict, that connection happens instantaneously and profoundly. I love alcoholics and addicts. They are my people, they are my tribe. They drive me crazy too. They're nuts, and they're excruciatingly difficult. But there's that connection.

So today, I have three kids who have never seen me drunk or stoned. Miracle, from where I come from. My children know absolutely what drugs and alcohol can do (not that drugs do it to everybody), but they know *they* have that genetic predisposition. As a society we've become much better educated and better at talking about it. Parents know how to talk about these issues, to a large extent, with their children.

One of the great gifts of my recovery is to have actually touched my humanity without being at the mercy of it: to realize who I am in the fullest way. I never thought like that when I was an addict. Finding recovery means I can think, *What do I have as an individual to offer the world?*

∽

Christopher Kennedy Lawford has spent much of his life in Hollywood and Washington, navigating these two worlds as an actor, writer, lawyer, activist, and public speaker. However, before his successes, Lawford battled a drug and alcohol addiction for much of his early life. In recovery for more than twenty-four years, he shares his experience, strength, and hope to make a difference in people's lives. He is the author of two books that have been on the New York Times *bestseller list:* Symptoms of Withdrawal *and* Moment of Clarity. *This story was excerpted from an interview by Mennonite producer/director Burton Buller with Mr. Lawford for a documentary,* Finding Hope in Recovery: Families Living With Addiction, *at www. FindingHopeInRecovery.com.*

3

Grace to Laugh

Hannah Heinzekehr

⁂

It had been raining on and off all day long. The floor of the bus was slick with rainwater brought in on people's shoes and dripping off of umbrellas and coats, and I felt my tennis shoes slide as I made my way to the back of the bus. It was five o'clock, and the bus was full of people heading home after a long day's work.

I did not feel like talking to anyone, but open seats proved scarce. I studiously avoided eye contact as I made my way down the aisle, eventually managing to find a seat next to a young girl, maybe about twelve or thirteen, still dressed in her bright blue school uniform and carrying a big bag of books on her lap. She had headphones stuffed into her ears and studiously stared out the tinted window. She would be the perfect seat partner, lost in her own world and not interested in conversation.

It had been a long day. I was tired and I could feel sadness beginning to creep into my bones and my mind. This morning's class had left me feeling frustrated and a bit hopeless. I was halfway through a fall semester studying in Derry (or Londonderry, depending on your Catholic or Protestant preferences), a city located in the north central part of Northern Ireland. Our program was focused on learning the history of "The Troubles" in Northern Ireland, and learning about methods of peacebuilding and conflict reconciliation that were being implemented by both Catholic and Protestant individuals. The day's discussion had focused on the current political stalemate in Northern Ireland (at the time, the two extremist parties were holding parliament hostage and no collaborative work could be done at the government level).

This dreary topic, combined with my previous knowledge of rifts that divided people throughout the city as well as a recent bout of homesickness for Indiana, had left me searching for some sign of hope and new beginnings in Derry. I couldn't understand how people living here could possibly be happy and go about their daily business, given their previous history and disagreements with each other that still led to divided cities and slowly emptying churches.

In addition, I had spent the afternoon bumbling through an interview with my soon-to-be boss for an internship at Corrymeela, a well-known peace and reconciliation center located along the coast. I had been all set to be at my most witty and impressive, making it clear that I was knowledgeable about peace work and well qualified for the job, but I found that I was out of my league. Now I was replaying several garbled answers and kicking myself for not sounding more intelligent and coherent.

While I was lost in these gloomy thoughts, the bus stopped and an old man near the front of the bus rose to get off. He was sharply dressed and carried himself with an air of dignity, although he moved slowly; it was clear from his posture that walking was getting to be difficult for him. When he finally reached the bus doors and they swung open, his nattily clad feet slipped on the wet floor of the bus. He lost his balance and toppled to the floor. He landed flat on his back with a sickening thud; for a moment, the entire bus fell silent, taking in what had just happened.

Then, two or three people sitting near the front of the bus leapt from their seats and hurried to help the man get back on his feet. Once he had righted himself, the man stood there for a moment surveying the the people on the bus with a somewhat shocked and embarrassed expression on his face. Then a strange thing happened. He threw his head back and began to laugh. He smiled and said out loud, but almost as if he were speaking to himself, "I must be moving on now. No sense dwelling on that." And with that he made his way out onto the sidewalk and into the rain.

I was struck by this man's fall, but more importantly, by his laughter. Here was grace. Perhaps this man exhibited a lesson the people of Northern Ireland know better than anyone. We fall, we get back up again, we laugh, we move on, and we offer ourselves grace. For without laughter, how could we survive our own shame?

This all happened in a moment—simply a matter of seconds—but it is a memory that has seared itself into my consciousness since that day. That bus ride back to my host home, as I gazed out at the rain-soaked roads, was not the first time that I have second-guessed myself and mentally chastised myself when things have not turned out the way I envisioned.

Typically, when I think about grace, I think about times when I have failed or fallen short of deserving something and others have offered grace and forgiveness to me, even though I didn't deserve these gifts. Or, on the other hand, I can be the bringer of grace when I'm willing to pardon someone else who has wronged me. Sometimes in the Christian sphere, we use *grace* interchangeably with *salvation*. It's a gift that comes from God and through Jesus Christ to undeserving but penitent humans. It cannot be earned, but is bestowed despite our lack of merit.

We do not often think about offering grace to ourselves; this may well be one of the hardest things that we are asked to do. For me, it is easier to reassure someone else in the wake of their own perceived shortcomings than it is to forgive myself when things don't work out as I plan—or when I embarrass myself by slipping up or falling down (both literally and figuratively).

The old man on the bus could have chosen to hang his head in shame. He could have scurried away from the bus doors and prying eyes as fast as possible, while mentally chastising himself for his clumsiness and lack of grace. But instead, he laughed and let himself off the hook. Similarly, I need to be willing to laugh at my own mistakes and to allow myself to breathe and recoup. Failing is part of being human, but so is offering ourselves the opportunity to move on and let go of these painful memories.

We fall, we get back up again, we laugh, and we move on. This is grace, too.

∞

Hannah Heinzekehr lives and works in Claremont, California, with her husband, Justin, and infant daughter, Elena. She works as the convention planning coordinator for Mennonite Church USA and reflects on life, theology, and being Mennonite at her blog, The Femonite. *In her spare time, she enjoys reading, hiking, going to the beach, and watching soccer. She spent a semester abroad in Northern Ireland as a student at Bluffton University.*

4

Parenting Scare

Jenn Esbenshade

⬤

*"A state of mind that sees God in everything is evidence
of growth in grace and a thankful heart."*
—Charles G. Finney

There's something about having children that creates a particular vulnerability in us. This little person is your heart, all that love and affection bubbling out to the surface. As parents we are left to watch this piece of our heart move about, unconnected from us, unable to shield it from all of life's dangers.

But in this journey of parenting, I have found that God's grace, God's unmerited help along the way, has sustained me. Often the daily episodes of life are colored by God's sometimes sneaky interventions. The comment from a friend heard at just the right time to change my mood. The verse in my Bible reading that I just happened to read at the right time. My spouse with the added measure of patience in the moment when I need it most. These are the times when we are apt to credit chance or happenstance instead of finding God in the details.

Grace was apparent the day that my two-year-old, Myla Grace, awoke from her nap. As I walked into her room, I immediately noticed that both eyes were pointing in toward her nose. As I stared in disbelief, Myla could only respond with a questioning "Mommy?" as she tried to understand why I was looking at her so strangely. I called my husband; then I called the doctor's office to find out what this meant and what we should do. It's remarkable how often it happens to be a late Friday afternoon when you realize your child needs to see a doctor.

As we waited for the doctor to call back with instructions, we began to convince ourselves that this wasn't a big deal. Finally, close to eight o'clock in the evening, the phone rang. The nurse was very calm and kind as she told me rather firmly that I needed to get Myla to the emergency room right away. Immediately I began to sob at the stupidity of waiting so long and the possibility of the irreparable harm we may have caused.

Of course, the ER was extremely busy that evening. My husband had stayed home with our son so I found myself alone and vulnerable. Feeling numb and helpless, I snuggled my little girl—my heart—curled up in my lap.

Since everything else was full, we were finally taken to a back waiting room that was being used as an exam room. The longer we sat, the more I became convinced that we were forgotten in this far reach of the hospital. Then the door opened and grace stepped through.

In my years of "staying home" with my children, I taught college Spanish courses as an adjunct professor. The one course I taught repeatedly was a Spanish class for nurses in a program that brought in students from many different counties and many different clinical settings. The classes were always small, and in the course of my teaching, I had maybe seventy-five students in total. The statistical likelihood that I would "run into" one of these students in their department, on their shift, at one of the many different hospitals and clinics in our area was next to impossible.

But there he stood. A familiar face just when I needed reassurance that my baby would be okay. As he did some basic neurological testing, he walked me through the many possibilities of why her eyes would just suddenly cross. He also explained that the ER was slammed that night and that with only two doctors on duty we would need to be patient.

When the doctor came in, I couldn't help but laugh at the sheer enormity of grace with which God reassured me in that moment. On the doctor's stethoscope I noticed a symbol for Mennonite Church USA: a distinctive green dove outline. Maybe it was silly, but as a Mennonite myself, this also felt reassuring and seemed to be a reminder of God's deep care for my child and for me.

That night we all learned that children's eyes can cross spontaneously when the muscles tire of working too hard for too long to keep them straight. A trip to a pediatric ophthalmologist on Monday and a pair of glasses fixed Myla's eyes. The lesson of God's abundant grace, however, extended far beyond that night.

God's divine plan has often been compared to a tapestry. From down below, we see only a jumble of strings that bear no pattern or symmetry, but from above those same disparate strings combine into a design of immeasurable beauty. Many long to see this finished picture of how the jumbled events of life will come together into a complete whole. The connections are woven together with God's grace, which somehow redeems even the most discouraging of life's events.

I too used to long to see how this life picture would come together in God's eye. I dreamed of seeing the trajectory of my life with each piece fitting neatly into place. And then I had children.

Suddenly I didn't want to see that complete picture because the enormity of it was just too much for this heart to bear. The pieces seemed too terrifying and I found myself standing on the only thing that remained—grace. For what is parenting but extending grace each day?

⌒

Jenn Esbenshade lives on an organic farm in New Holland, Pennsylvania, with her husband, Wade, and her two children, Davin and Myla. During the school year she teaches first grade in the Spanish Immersion program at Lancaster Mennonite School, and in the summer she runs her family's produce stand. She is a member of New Holland Mennonite Church.

5

You Are All One

Ryan Dueck

Several years ago, when I was a freshly minted seminary graduate in my first year of pastoral ministry, I received an unexpected lesson in the strange and delightful places and ways that grace appears in our world.

One morning I was the guest speaker at another church in our denomination. It was a community comprised mainly of well-educated white-collar types. The worship service was formal and highly structured with a strong sense of reverence and propriety. There was beautiful artwork throughout the sanctuary and a high degree of musical skill evident in the singing.

The theme of the service was "called to community" on Galatians 3:26-29. My sermon was not very complicated. The basic idea was that the shape of the Christian community we are called to is one where all are welcome, regardless of race, gender, socioeconomic status, age. The message seemed to be very well received and I had several stimulating, enjoyable conversations after the service.

Usually I would depart from guest speaking engagements in those first years with an overwhelming sense of relief that I had simply survived and not made a fool of myself, but on that day I actually enjoyed the experience with a minimal amount of anxiety. It was a good morning.

Later in the day I was back in my hometown for two worship services with inmates at the local correctional center. Obviously this was a very different worship experience than the one I had been part of earlier in the day. The inmates trickled in wearing their red coveralls—an obvious and omnipresent reminder of their "separateness" from the rest of us—and took their seats in the sparsely decorated chapel. A few songs were sung, mostly off-key and with varying degrees of enthusiasm. Two of the prisoners stumbled through the Scripture readings; the chaplain delivered an informal homily; there was a prayer time, followed by a few more songs and a benediction. At the end, there was time for cookies and coffee, hurriedly stuffed in over conversation before the guard arrived to lead the inmates back to their cells.

And yet, in Galatians 3:28 (NIV) Paul writes: "All of you are one in Christ Jesus." On one level, the world of the inmates and the world of the congregation I was in earlier that day didn't *seem* to be "one." Paul speaks of how the lines we use to divide ourselves have been abolished in Christ. But they still felt pretty real that day. We still have very clear categories, even in the church. Educated/uneducated, white-collar/blue-collar, formal/informal, volunteer/inmate, inside/outside. Whatever unity Christ has made possible among human beings seemed more of a future hope than a present reality to me as I reflected on these very different experiences.

But there are moments when we get a glimpse of this future hope breaking into the present. Even in our world full of divisions and suspicions, grace shows up in the cracks. In the second service at the correctional center, as a part of his homily, the chaplain had read the inmates a story from CNN about a little girl in Afghanistan who spent six hours a day begging for bread because her dad was strung out on drugs and couldn't/wouldn't provide for his wife and daughters. It was a heartbreaking story, but made little perceptible impact at the time of its reading.

Or so I thought. During the prayer time, one large, red-faced young man boomed out the following prayer:

> *Hi, God. It's Tyler again. I'm getting out on Tuesday and I need you to help me make it this time. I need you to fill me up and show me the way that I need to go, to protect me and those I love. Please watch over me, God.*
>
> *And God, please give this girl in Afghanistan some bread. I work in the kitchen, and I know that we throw a lot of bread in the garbage every day. It's terrible and we shouldn't do it. The amount of bread we throw out each day could probably feed a whole village. I don't know, God, she needs some of our bread. Just please, give this little girl some bread.*

It was one of those precious, grace-soaked moments when the truth and the power of the kingdom came shining through, when our common humanity seemed much stronger and more enduring than the walls and divisions we put in place to keep us apart. I preached about oneness in Christ in the morning but the real sermon came later in the day when I witnessed one simple, practical expression of how the love of Christ can break down the walls between human beings.

All of you are one in Christ Jesus. Really?

Really. You are all one.

Those jetting off to accept postdoctoral fellowships, and those behind bars for the fifth time in the last ten years. Those whose prayers are eloquent and rich in theological truth, and those just desperately seeking help in making it on the outside this time. Those who sing majestic hymns in beautiful four-part harmony, and those who can't hold a tune and lurch halfheartedly through a simple chorus. Those who worship in clean, comfortable, and aesthetically pleasing sanctuaries, and those who sit on plastic chairs in a concrete room with little more than an old piano and a simple wooden cross on the wall. Those with bread to spare, and those who need them to spare it.

∞

Ryan Dueck lives in southern Alberta, Canada, with his wife, Naomi, and twins, Claire and Nicholas. He blogs at www.rynomi.wordpress.com and is currently helping to lead a small Mennonite church that seeks to embody the peace, simplicity, and hope of the gospel of Christ in a noisy and conflicted culture. As all good Canadians must, he loves ice hockey, as well as soccer, good books, good coffee, motorcycles, and mountains.

6

The Teacup

Alan Stucky

⌒

Shortly after I began pastoring at a church in 2009 in Harper, Kansas, I met several members who had lived in Bolivia while working with Mennonite Central Committee (MCC) in the 1980s. They had helped our church begin to connect with churches around Santa Cruz, Bolivia, first simply praying for each other. Out of that the church in Kansas took several service trips to Santa Cruz, but mainly to simply build a mutual relationship between the churches in Kansas and Santa Cruz.

In 2010, I accompanied our youth group on a service trip to work at the *Guarderia Samuelito* (Little Samuel Daycare), a project started by the Mennonite churches in Santa Cruz. That trip was a wonderful introduction and it left me with the strong feeling that our church needed to deepen our relationships. So for several weeks we hosted Leonidas Saucedo (Ona), one of the pastors from the Bolivian Mennonite Church, in Kansas. During that time my wife said to me, "I may regret saying this, but when you take sabbatical time next year, I think you need to go to Bolivia."

Even though this would mean that we would be apart for almost six weeks, she too recognized the importance of strengthening these relationships, both for me and for our church. And so I began talking with my congregation, making plans, and attempting a crash course in Spanish.

At last, I kissed my wife goodbye and made the trek to Santa Cruz. Upon arriving I was greeted warmly by the fiancé of a young man in our church and Pastor Ona and his children. They knew very little English and I knew very little Spanish, but nevertheless we greeted each other with hugs and kisses. Upon arriving at Ona's house his wife showed me to my room: a room that happens to be the only room in the house with air-conditioning. As she was fixing lunch, she told me that if I wanted anything to just help myself because she was more comfortable when her guests felt at home. Overall, it was one of the warmest receptions I've ever had.

Over the course of the following weeks, I found out that the reception I had received from Ona and his family was not out of the ordinary and was not simply because we had a prior relationship. Day after day I met new people, many times being received into their homes. Time after time I was welcomed with open arms and a joyful spirit. The pinnacle of this came when I was invited to go with the rest of the family to Ona's mother's house.

On Sunday evenings Ona's family gathers together to visit and bake bread, a tradition loaded with personal family significance. The house itself was rather modest—nice by Bolivian standards—but to the North American eye would seem very humble. I, feeling like a big goof gringo, followed Ona into the courtyard where everyone was gathered. After greeting everyone, it felt as though attention quickly turned to me. I was invited to sit in one of the chairs, though there weren't enough for everyone. They placed a table next to me along with a plate piled high with freshly baked sweet bread and spicy cornbread biscuits. I was encouraged to start eating as many of them as I could, and they asked if I would like some coffee or tea. I said that I'd love some coffee.

After munching on a few of the warm biscuits, I was offered a white teacup complete with matching saucer. As the young woman handed me the teacup, I realized that I had just been given what was quite possibly the nicest piece of china that they had in the entire house. Here I was, a stranger who simply showed up unannounced in their home, and I was given the best of what they had to offer. It was not simply that I had been welcomed into their home during an intimate family moment. Rather, they had rolled out the red carpet for me. As the stranger I had become the honored guest. The truly humbling realization was that this was not out of the ordinary. Everywhere I had been, I had become the honored guest. The fatted calf had been killed in my honor. My impression was that I had not been a special "stranger," but that all guests would be treated with a similar reception.

In Matthew 25 Jesus says, "I was a stranger and you welcomed me" (NRSV). I have come to realize that while I have believed hospitality to be a mandate for all Christians, in the past I have responded only with the bare minimum. Too often I have simply tolerated the presence of the stranger as an obligation, rather than seeking out the stranger to serve him or her with joy and with the best that I have.

∽

Alan Stucky is the pastor at Pleasant Valley Mennonite Church in Harper, Kansas. After graduating from Goessel High School, he went to Bethel College in North Newton, Kansas, where he met his wife, Katie. After graduating with a BA in Bible and religion, he began working at Buhler Mennonite Church in Buhler, Kansas. While working at Buhler Mennonite Church, he began studies at Associated Mennonite Biblical Seminary. After graduating in 2009 with an MDiv, he moved to Harper, Kansas.

Bridge

7

Softened by Grace

Melodie Miller Davis

∽

When I was seventeen and about to embark on my senior year of high school, my family packed up the car, a pickup truck, and U-haul trailer and moved nine hundred miles from Indiana to north Florida.

Northern Florida was light years away from south Florida in terms of the beach culture of Fort Lauderdale or Miami. North Florida was more like living in very rural Georgia or Alabama: Deep South in everything from accents to attitudes.

The year was 1969: the Vietnam War was in full swing; it was the first year of full racial integration of public schools; and just a year after Robert Kennedy and Martin Luther King Jr. had been shot, for reasons not unrelated.

So I was the new girl in school. I can still remember one boy glaring at me and spitting out, "Damn Yankee. We don't need any more of ya'll down here. If we could fight the war again, we'd win this time." And it was not the Vietnam War he was talking about.

We had a government class called "Americanism versus Communism," and every day the teacher, Mr. Dickens [name changed], would rant about g'vment, religion, freedom, the fortunes of University of Alabama football, and huntin'.

Not only was I new and freshly imported from the North, but I was immediately categorized as Mennonite. Everyone knew Mennonites were different. Some of the local Mennonites were different in dress, but others like me were different mainly because of our beliefs.

I had lived a sheltered life near Goshen, Indiana, where most of my friends, teachers, and neighbors were either Mennonite, Brethren, Amish, or Conservative Mennonite. I went to the Mennonite high school my first three years and enjoyed a great bunch of friends. My biggest crisis was breaking up with my steady boyfriend shortly before we moved.

So even though initially I was excited about the move, once there I felt isolated, lonely, and very different from most of my peers. For the first time in my life, I hated and dreaded school.

Mr. Dickens had a chip on his shoulder when it came to religious people. Mostly, he thought they were a bunch of hypocrites: "Fiiine Babtists (his pronounciation) on Sunday morning, but who do you find drinkin' and drivin' home from Joe's Bar on a Saturday night? Whoohie!"

Still, as a new southern transplant, I was fascinated with his stories. What high schooler wasn't content to listen to tall tales and loud opinions for an hour rather than buckling down to discussing the assigned reading? At times his logic and opinions made sense, and I realized his mind went deeper than huntin' dogs and 'Bama football. He was, after all, editor of the town paper.

Mr. Dickens picked up early on my faith background and would buttonhole me with questions like "How would Mennonites keep Communists from taking over our country if it ever came to that?" I remember my face feeling hot as I stumbled for answers. I was raised to be a "nice" girl, so I never thought of it as bullying or badgering or a hostile classroom environment.

In our Mennonite family, one of the firm rules guiding our lives was that Sunday was a day of rest. We only did the necessary chores of taking care of animals—and "women's work" of cooking and washing dishes. Dad, as a rule, would never drive a tractor or do any work that could wait until Monday.

But in Calhoun County, a day of rest for humans was also a day when hunters would take their huntin' dogs and go scouting for deer.

One Sunday afternoon in the fall, when the ground was soggy and full from the hurricane season, Dad could hear a vehicle stuck in the mud across the fields. You could hear the tires whirring in the mud. So Dad went out quietly and got his tractor, fetched some sturdy chains, and went rambling down the paths between fields until he reached the source of the sound.

Who did he find there but Mr. Dickens and his dogs, with his truck stuck up to its axles.

Dad quickly pulled Mr. Dickens's truck out of the mud. I don't know if Dad worried about whether neighbors would think he was working on Sunday when they saw him on his tractor. But Dad did tell me he'd found and freed my government teacher.

On Monday morning, Mr. Dickens began class with, "I was out huntin' with my hounds Red and Rowdy yesterday . . ." and we settled in for what we hoped would be a long diversion from civics, government, and religion.

"Well, I was out near about the Miller farm," he said with a nod to me. "And then Whoohie! Fooey! Hot dang! The ole' truck jes mired down and wadn't going nowhere, no way. I rocked it back and forth. Of course, it jes made the mud worse, and I knew that, but what was I to do? I was eight miles from town.

"And then I looked up and who did I see puttin' across the fields but Mr. Miller, on his tractor, *on a Sunday*. And he commenced to putting his chains on my truck and had me out of there in no time at all.

"Now that's a fine Christian man who don't ker what his neighbors will think, that he's disobeying the rule about not working on Sunday to help this poor ole teacher out of the mud."

He turned to me. "I'll never forget that, Miz Miller. You've got a fine father. If everybody who went to church was like that, we'd all be better off. Now that's what Christian love is all about. You tell him thank you ag'in for me now, will you?"

And Mr. Dickens never did forget my father's simple act of kindness. He brought it up often in our discussions of religion the rest of the year. I felt less "on trial" and less suspect in my faith tradition.

Dad's bridge of grace to help someone in a ditch in spite of normal Sunday rules softened the opinion of a curmudgeonly teacher that day—and maybe of this young self-righteous northerner who needed to open herself to be more accepting of anyone, no matter what kind of opinions they expressed or where they lived. I doubt Dad thought of himself as extending grace when he went to get his tractor, but Mr. Dickens's ideas about Christians, pacifists, and Mennonites would never be quite as hardened.

∞

Melodie M. Davis is a writer/producer for MennoMedia in Harrisonburg, Virginia. She writes the syndicated newspaper column Another Way *and is the author of eight books, most recently* Whatever Happened to Dinner? Recipes and Reflections for Family Mealtime *(2010: Herald Press). Melodie also keeps a blog, www.FindingHarmonyBlog .com. She and her husband, Stuart, are members of Trinity Presbyterian Church in Harrisonburg, a house-church based congregation, and are parents of three adult daughters.*

8

They Loved Him Back

Lynda Hollinger-Janzen

∞

*John Powell, a Mennonite pastor and Mennonite agency
staff worker for many years, recalls a confrontation his
father, John Sidney, had with Ku Klux Klan members
in 1948.*

John Sidney had sold some lumber cut on his farm near
Hissop, Alabama, to a Klan member who paid with a
check calculated to bounce. John Sidney refused to keep
quiet about this injustice. When he learned that a pickup
of armed Klansmen was headed toward his home, John
Sidney sent his seven-year-old son, also named John, to the
safety of a neighbor's house and laid plans.

As the pickup pulled in front of the Powell home, the
fraudulent check writer yelled an obscenity-laced command for John Sidney to present himself. John Sidney did.
He stepped out of the door with composure—and two
firearms.

One of the Klansmen barked a command to drop the guns, to which John Sidney replied, "You better look around before you go any further."

The noisy bravado of the men in the pickup died into silence as they became aware of John Sidney's wife, Willie Mae, standing at a window with her rifle trained on one Klansmen; sons and relatives with more guns were poised at each window, on the roof, and behind trees.

The hush was broken as the pickup sputtered to life and backed off the Powell property. Soon, there was only a cloud of exhaust left to indicate that the Klan had been there. A few days later, John Sidney received full payment for the lumber in cash.

⚬⚬

"I didn't grow up with a pacifist heritage," John Powell reflects. "It was a slow conversion from violence to nonviolence as I was around people who were practicing peace. I saw a change in people and the mood of the nation when protests were nonviolent."

Powell was in high school when he first spoke with Martin Luther King Jr. Over the next four years, he became a conscientious objector under King's mentoring.

"That was one of the things Martin taught, that you could be affirming of those who are your enemies," Powell says. "He also said if we were COs [conscientious objectors], we needed to connect ourselves to a historic peace church."

Of the peace church options, Powell chose Mennonites because of the voluntary service workers he'd encountered and worked alongside in three Michigan locations. One of these workers, Shirley Hochstedler of Kokomo, Indiana, later became Powell's wife and partner in ministry.

Racism was not only present in society. It followed John to a position working for the Minority Ministries Council

for the Mennonite church. "Granted, I was a little radical.
I did not wear a suit and tie. I wore my dashikis [West
African traditional garb]. I had the pulpit on the level of the
congregation and rearranged the rows of pews so they were
facing each other. I also organized a reconciliation center
on the site where the Wichita [Kansas] riots had just happened," Powell says.

Powell's ministry in Wichita lasted one year before he
was invited to become executive secretary of the Minority
Ministries Council in Elkhart, Indiana. In this capacity,
he worked on a document that suggested concrete ways
of empowering Mennonite congregations in African-
American, Hispanic, and Native American communities
across the U.S. In 1969, Powell presented his proposals at a
churchwide meeting in Turner, Oregon.

"If I thought I had hell before, I had more," Powell says.
"A brother got up in the meeting and said, 'If we do what
John Powell says to do, the next thing they'll have me out
of my pulpit and a nigger in there.'"

After five years of trying to work within the racist struc-
tures of the Mennonite church, Powell was angry and discouraged. "I left the Mennonite church declaring clearly
that I would never ever return," Powell says.

However, over the next two decades, as Powell min-
istered in several denominations in the United States and
internationally, he made his way, step by step, back to the
Mennonite church he loved so much.

"I was evangelized back into the Mennonite church,"
Powell says. "It was brothers and sisters who loved me to
death. They invited me to meetings. They listened to me.
They became increasingly involved in the struggle for civil
rights."

Throughout his life, Powell has practiced the ministry
of reconciliation he preaches—even to the extent of accepting the man as "brother" who was once his Oregon conference critic. In Kenya, during a conference that Powell
organized to encourage dialogue between African and

African-American theologians, he was christened Sebsebe Samantar—the Gatherer and Peacemaker. In the former Soviet Union, a Russian Christian presented him with a special cross, and John viewed it as symbolic of the tremendous changes that had occurred in his life as he found his new calling and identity. He now has an extensive collection of crosses and would still rather wear them than a suit or necktie.

Now, finally retired, John has brought courage, passion, and "seventy-times-seven forgiveness" to his ministry. He inherited some of these qualities; the rest, he says, is a gift of God's grace.

∞

John Powell has served pastorates and worked in a variety of agency, university, and church settings since the '60s. In 1995, he accepted a half-time position as director of evangelism and church development with Mennonite Board of Missions, while he continued to teach and provide administration for a ministry training program at Houghton College in western New York. Powell served in various director capacities with the mission agency that became Mennonite Mission Network in 2002. In semiretirement, he worked as a church relations associate and mission advocate and now enjoys real retirement.

Lynda Hollinger-Janzen is a writer for Mennonite Mission Network.

9

Walking the Jesus Trail

Sarah Thompson

It was just a few more kilometers to walk to the hostel where Elizabeth (Liz) and I planned to stay the night. We saw that we had to pass alongside an Israeli military base. The "Jesus Trail" guidebook warned us to keep out of the area. We breathed a prayer that we'd make it past all right. This was our first day walking the Jesus Trail; we had departed from Nazareth that morning and had stopped in the legendary town of Cana for lunch. What a day, walking in the footsteps of the Messiah, seeing the countryside and landscapes that nurtured him.

As we plotted our way along the edge of the military base, we could see old army trucks in the distance and soldiers walking and lounging around them. We were almost past the military base when we heard shouts and whistles coming at us from behind, where there were army trucks and Israeli soldiers.

We stopped and looked back. I looked at Liz, terrified. She grinned. My experience overseas told me that if you are two young women in a new place you don't know, being summoned by a group of men with automatic weapons, you just wave and keep walking in the opposite direction.

I couldn't convince Liz that maybe this situation was not very safe; she was determined to hear an Israeli military perspective on the regional situation. I was nervous because we'd just come from visiting the Christian Peacemaker Teams' office in the heated surroundings of Hebron/Al-Khalil, and as we'd traveled from Jerusalem north to Galilee, everyone was on edge because of a recent incident.

Liz reminded me that God was in charge, and since we were on the Jesus Trail, we ought to do what Jesus would do. He would talk to the soldiers. I looked at her hard. We turned back toward the whistles and shouts still floating in our direction. We settled on a code word that either of us could say in case we felt unsafe—a signal to leave immediately. I took in the surroundings—the high bushes, the army equipment, the setting sun—and muttered Psalm 19:14, "Let the words of my mouth and the meditations of my heart be acceptable to you, O LORD, my rock and my redeemer."

The soldiers were quite enthused that we approached. The ones who spoke English translated for the others who did not, and they pounced on us with questions.

"Where do you come from?"

"Nazareth . . . er, the United States and Canada."

"What are your names?"

"Sarah and Elizabeth."

"Ah, good Jewish names! Are you Jewish?"

"We are on a pilgrimage, following in the footsteps of Jesus. We want to learn more about his life."

"Do you want some tuna?" one offered and then added, "You're the first women we've seen in two weeks!" (I thought about saying the code word right at that moment, but Liz jumped in with a question for them.)

"When you are done with these training exercises and are on duty, where are you posted?" she asked.

"Hebron," they answered. "Do you know of it?"

Gulp. We'd already been sternly instructed by the Israeli Border Patrol not to go into the West Bank. Should we reveal to these soldiers that we had disobeyed their government in order to visit our friends? "Yes, we've heard of it," I stammered quickly. Then I asked for some tuna.

That lifted the mood a bit. They were quite excited to feed us, and we were ready to eat after our all-day walk. So we broke bread together. We ate from their enormous foodstuffs of tuna, peanuts, Israeli Nutella, Gatorade-like energy powder that turned water pink, bean paste, and sliced bread. We ate our fill, and they chuckled and murmured among themselves as we ate.

Once an older soldier understood that we were going to be walking for the next few days (our destination was Capernaum), he climbed into the back of the truck and pulled out even more food. He insisted we load our bags. "We have enough tuna to last us six months!" he beamed.

"*Todah!*" I said, trying to say thank you in Hebrew and make a gracious exit. "Oh, do you speak Hebrew?" the translating soldier asked. "Well," I hesitated, "I learned a little bit of ancient Hebrew in school."

"Say some more!" another soldier requested. I sat back down. There were plenty of things I desired to say to members of the Israeli Defense Force. Among other things, they are infamous for brutal Palestinian home invasions and routine child arrests in the name of settler protection in the occupied Palestinian Territories. Thinking about their role in this tangled situation caused me much despair and anger. But those angry words weren't coming to me. All that emerged in my mind was one assignment from Basic Hebrew class. We memorized a short passage. I had chosen part of the Ten Commandments (Deuteronomy 5:12-14, 17-20). So I shared that with them:

"Observe the sabbath day and keep it holy, as the Lord your God commanded you. Six days you shall labor and do all your work. But the seventh day is a sabbath to the Lord your God; you shall not do any work—you, or your son or your daughter, or your male or female slave, or your ox or your donkey, or any of your livestock, or the resident alien in your towns, so that your male and female slave may rest as well as you."

They *seemed* impressed (I couldn't quite tell). Liz licked some of the Nutella-like substance off of her fingers. I smiled and continued slowly, recognizing that the words that I was about to share with them were words for all of us to hear. And they would probably resonate deeper than any words I could have thought of to convince the members of the Israeli army to lay down their weapons and know those things that make for peace. They were words—commandments even—from the God we both worship. I continued in Hebrew:

"You shall not kill. Neither shall you commit adultery. Neither shall you steal. Neither shall you bear false witness against your neighbor . . ."

There was a moment—we all looked at each other. Sephardic and Ashkenazi Jews, brown and white North American Christians. Then the moment got awkward and another question pierced the silence. Nonetheless, it was clear to me that God indeed had graciously answered my prayer and guided the words of my mouth that evening, as I had the courage to engage my enemies and speak God's message of challenge and grace.

◌◌

Sarah Thompson is a scholar-activist from Elkhart, Indiana. She received an MDiv from Anabaptist Mennonite Biblical Seminary before working at Sabeel Jerusalem (2011–12) through Mennonite Central Committee. She has been formed by her roots in Elkhart and her travels to five continents through volunteer work with Mennonite World Conference, feminist antiwar movements, women's soccer teams, the Fulbright Scholarship, and Spelman College. She is currently a fundraising assistant for the Society for Menstrual Cycle Research and the outreach coordinator for Christian Peacemaker Teams, an organization that does strategic nonviolent intervention in areas of lethal conflict.

10

An Unfinished Part

Lou Gomez Jr., as told to Elizabeth Raid

∞

When I was growing up I wanted to be a priest, but I couldn't reconcile that call with my desire to also have a family. While raising a family, I had a conversion experience and was rebaptized. I became involved in a large, nondenominational congregation where I served as a lay minister working with children and families, and as a deacon, doing street ministry. When my employment in a challenging work environment at a local factory ended, I began to wonder what else God had in mind for me.

Without a job, I accepted an opportunity to travel with a church-related group to Africa to learn more about how God was working through people to help those affected by AIDS. That led to a desire to enter pastoral ministry studies. Because of family expectations, I had never had the opportunity for college. When I thought about what was happening as I began college, I remembered the words of a song my grandfather sang in Spanish: "There really ought to be a sign upon my heart: don't touch me yet; there's an unfinished part."

After graduation I was called to a church in a small rural city that had some younger people who passed through and after a year or two they would move on to other areas. Aging members also moved or passed on. With them went much of the energy needed for community outreach and vision.

On Saturday mornings, I would sit in the back of the sanctuary and spend time in prayer, asking God to fill this place with his Spirit and light. *Of course, filling the pews would be fine too, Lord*, I prayed. After months—even several years—I wondered if God had given up on this small congregation. And what about me, Lord?

Then God surprised me with grace again. One Saturday I realized someone had entered the sanctuary. When I looked up, I saw two men who looked like they could be my brothers standing nearby. They introduced themselves as Christians. One of the men explained that he had been leading weekly Bible study and prayer for several years. They were looking for a place to rent that could accommodate their growing group. They felt God had led them to this Mennonite church that they passed on their way to and from work each day.

Several months later, when our two congregations reached a rental agreement, we began sharing the building. The traditional church kept their usual meeting times, and the Spanish-speaking group met for their Spanish worship on Sunday afternoons. Growing up in a Catholic, Spanish-speaking home and leaving the Catholic church and embracing Anabaptism, I had much in common with this new group of believers. Over meals and conversations with the Hispanic church pastor and his wife, my wife and I shared how our Anabaptist Mennonite beliefs shape our values and inform our discipleship. We gave them Spanish translations of all the writings on these subjects that we could find.

There were many challenges for me in this role. The traditional congregation had called me to be their pastor. Now I felt God asking more of me. How could I keep my commitment to that congregation, yet minister to the needs of the Hispanic group? I felt pulled in several directions and had to think about who my real boss was!

Through the Spirit's leading, our continued building of relationships, and very helpful mentoring and training by the Hispanic pastor for our district Mennonite conference, this new congregation is vibrant and growing. Last summer our district conference recognized them as a church plant.

The traditional congregation remains firm in its faith, although small in numbers. There are many challenges to building bridges across language, culture, and different expectations of these two congregations. While we share the same God, the same Lord Jesus Christ as Savior, the same baptism, and the same blessing of the Holy Spirit, how we express that faith and live it may differ greatly.

Through fellowship meals shared on special occasions, informal conversations, and much prayer, we are beginning to listen to and learn from each other. God's Spirit is continuing to work in the lives of individual church members and in the shared life of these two congregations.

When I remember the words from that song my grandfather sang so often, "Don't take me yet; there's an unfinished part," I know that God's grace continues to help me grow through opportunities to listen, encourage, and learn what that unfinished part might look like. The song Grandfather sang goes on and on. It is never finished. The refrain continues when God's grace gets passed on from generation to generation. As a grandfather myself to thirteen young grandchildren, I will keep that song alive in my own life and in whatever ways God gives me as I minister to others across languages, cultures, and customs.

∽

Lou Gomez Jr. grew up in Newton, Kansas, where he has lived most of his life. His pastoral duties take him to

Liberal, Kansas, a four-hour, one-way commute, where he serves Calvary Mennonite Church. He continues to work to strengthen relationships between Calvary and Camino de Santidad and occasionally assists Camino with pastoral duties. During the week, he works at Offender Victim Ministry where he counsels people referred by the court for anger management and shoplifting. Although he enjoys singing, he prefers to play softball and other sports with his eleven grandsons and two granddaughters.

Elizabeth Raid is a freelance writer who writes frequently for Rejoice! *magazine.*

Grace Beyond Death

11

Grace for Sally Elsie

Owen E. Burkholder

∞

For thirteen years we enjoyed knowing Sally Elsie and "Jimmie." We moved into the parsonage (a house in the church parking lot) when our first daughter, Minnette, was a few months old and I was beginning my second year at Eastern Mennonite Seminary in Harrisonburg, Virginia.

Jimmie and Elsie lived across Green Street and became surrogate grandparents to our daughters. Jimmie was a World War II veteran who would never speak of what he had experienced during the war. While he was overseas, his young bride took up with another man and Jimmie vowed never to marry again. He worked for many years with the Virginia Department of Transportation, maintaining the roads in the summer and plowing snow in the winter. He gave every appearance of being a weathered old man, but he showed only kindness to us and our children.

Elsie worked for many years in several of the sewing factories in Harrisonburg and did the cooking and housework for Jimmie in his retirement. Many times we would cross the street to sit on the front porch with Jimmie and Elsie. Elsie would serve her sweet tea (so strong it kept me awake at night) and other treats. As Baby Marla, and soon thereafter Michelle, joined our family, they were cared for by our neighbors. Often the girls would say, "Let's go visit Jimmie and Elsie." One particular evening it was raining hard when our little tribe made its way across the street. We learned later that when Jimmie heard the doorbell he said, "It's either the ducks or the Mennonites!"

My wife, Ruth Ann Augsburger, grew up in a church-planting family in Youngstown, Ohio. And I grew up in a church-planting family in northern Alberta, Canada. So, relating to non-Mennonite neighbors was all we knew. Jimmie and Elsie never did cross the street to come to church. But they were watching our family closely.

When I was invited to become pastor at a different church, Park View Mennonite, we moved a mile and a half away into a home of our own. Jimmie and Elsie said they missed us in the neighborhood. We kept in contact but less regularly.

One midnight, the phone rang and it was a nurse from the intensive care unit of the local hospital saying that Elsie, strapped to a respirator and dialysis machinery, had written a note asking to see "Reverend Burkholder." She had written, ". . . want to join church." I asked the nurse if she was stable, and when she replied affirmatively, I told her to tell Elsie that I would pick up Jimmie in the morning and come to see her; if she deteriorated over the night, the nurse should please call me back.

Next morning I told Jimmie and he went with me to the hospital. So, with Jimmie beside me and the ICU nurse at the foot of the bed watching, I began to talk with Elsie. I said, "They gave me your note saying you want to join church. I take that to mean that you would like to have a clear relationship with Jesus before you die." With all the tubes, she couldn't speak but she nodded her head. I then told her I would pray a prayer and if it was what she wanted to pray, I would keep my eyes open and she should nod as we went along. So I prayed a prayer of confession (head nodding), receiving the love of Jesus (head nodding), and gratitude (head nodding). Then, with Jimmie and the nurse watching, I asked Elsie if she would like to be baptized? Head nodded. I went over to a sink and got a handful of water, poured it over her very warm forehead with another prayer and welcomed "Sister Elsie" into the family of faith.

On the way home, I said to Jimmie, "Elsie made her peace with God today." He made no comment.

Elsie died four days later and I had the privilege of sharing in her funeral. Jimmie lived for several years after that. I visited him in the nursing home and often prayed with him including the night before he died. I also did his funeral with a burial on a rural hillside with grazing sheep looking on.

Long-term grace for Elsie, Jimmie, and for me. I'm looking forward to seeing them again someday.

∞

Owen E. Burkholder was born and raised in Bluesky, Alberta, Canada. After high school, Owen attended Ontario Mennonite Bible Institute, Kitchener, Ontario, where he first met Ruth Ann Augsburger. Following a BA from the University of Alberta, Edmonton, Owen did volunteer youth ministry in Youngstown, Ohio, where he and Ruth Ann were married December 31, 1971. In the fall of 1972, Owen and Ruth Ann moved to Harrisonburg, Virginia, to attend Eastern Mennonite Seminary. Over the past forty-one years Owen was pastor at Community Mennonite, Park View Mennonite, and served as conference minister for Virginia Mennonite Conference in Harrisonburg. Owen and Ruth Ann are parents of three and grandparents of three.

12

Surprised by Grace

Carol Penner

❦

As a pastor, I've had quite a few opportunities to visit the bedside of someone who is dying. These have been some of the most profound experiences of my ministry. But some of those visits have been harder than others—surprising in unsettling ways.

I was called to the bedside of one of my church members who was dying. This woman, whom I knew well, had been a bitter and opinionated person for as long as I'd known her. I had been visiting her pretty regularly in the last months, and as far as I could tell she was continuing down the path she had always taken. She was dying with much unfinished business and many broken relationships.

She had a daughter who was estranged from her; they had not spoken in ten years. There was a whole section of the family that she had no respect for, and she was leaving them out of her will. It was a bad business. All of my attempts to encourage her to think more redemptively about some of these relationships had ended in failure.

Part of the unfinished business was this woman's relationship with me. While she was mostly pleasant to my face, she had said some nasty things about me to several different people. She would shake my hand and smile as she left our church services, but I heard from a family member that she always tore a strip out of my sermons and declared that our church needed a better minister.

As a minister, you hear these second- and third-hand reports sometimes. Stories get back to you. Sometimes you choose to address them, and sometimes you choose to let them go. If someone has enough of an issue with you, they will confront you themselves, and then you can deal with it. In this case, knowing that the way this woman treated me was no different than the way she treated most people, I didn't make an issue of it. She certainly had issues that were bigger and more serious than her issues with me.

As the end drew nearer, this woman was still very clear in her mind. I had a chance to talk to some of the relatives who were gathering. They had hope that there might be a moment of grace at the end, and that some final peace might be found with her. So far, she had refused to see certain people.

As I drove to this pastoral visit with my dying church member, I knew that this would probably be my last visit. I knew that we needed a miracle. We needed grace in a big way—we needed some dramatic changes in a short time. And since I knew this person, and knew her personality, I knew what a big miracle I was asking for. As I turned off the car outside her house, I paused at the steering wheel and prayed, "God, send your Holy Spirit down. We really need it here!"

My visit with the woman was similar to many other visits; her voice was more feeble, but there was still the litany of complaints, the blame on everyone else. I asked her whether she would like to make peace with some of the people gathered. She declared snappishly that she had no unfinished business and that she had no apologies to make.

She was lying in the bed; I was sitting in a chair next to the bed. As I listened to her, frustration and hopelessness about lost chances flooded me, and I felt a wave of dislike for her. And then something happened.

I can only describe it like a *whoosh*; it was definitely a physical sensation. I was suddenly and completely filled with love for this woman, from top to bottom. As I looked at her, she was suddenly someone who was incredibly dear to me. She was so entirely loveable.

I had been sitting on a chair a few feet away from the bed but now I immediately went and knelt by the bed and held her hand. I put my other hand on her head and prayed with her, a prayer of fervent blessing, wishing her well on her way. I kissed her goodbye on her forehead, and she responded by saying, "Thank you, dear." Immediately, the home-care nurse came in and said that the time for our visit was over, since she was so weak. I stumbled from the room and out of the house. I sat in the car, shaking.

"What was that? What was that?" I asked myself. I had asked the Holy Spirit to show up, and the Holy Spirit had arrived. I just hadn't thought that I was the one who needed grace. I hadn't realized how much my own spirit needed to change.

I need to tell you that this was not a warm and comfortable thing that happened. It was an excruciating experience where I became acutely aware of how far I am from God in a lot of the work that I do; so often performing the motions of ministry, but without the love that ministry requires. My own sin so often gets in the way. This was a falling-on-your-knees-at-the-cross experience. I am thankful for the Spirit's chastising presence, for grace at the moment where it was so desperately needed.

The woman died around an hour after I left. She did not speak words of peace with any of the people waiting in the house downstairs.

I don't know what was in this woman's heart at the end. What I do know for certain, is that God was there showing grace to her at the end. Part of the grace came through me. I am sure it came through others who visited her as well. Did she deserve it? Do any of us deserve it? Perhaps that's the definition of grace: getting what we don't deserve.

That experience, and others, less dramatic perhaps but of a similar nature, have made me less blithe or casual about invoking the Spirit. They have made me more aware of the power of grace to change us.

To change me. Thanks be to God!

∞

Carol Penner is a pastor at The First Mennonite Church in Vineland, Ontario. She writes a blog of worship resources at www.leadinginworship.com.

13

Terminal Grace

Nancy Witmer

∞

For me, 2012 was the most difficult of times; it was the most blessed of times.

The difficult time actually started two years earlier when my brother, Earl, was diagnosed with Glioblastoma Multiforme (GBM). In layman's terms: grade 4 brain cancer. The neurosurgeon threw out grim statistics and told us there was no cure for this cancer, only treatment to slow its growth. Surgery, radiation, and chemotherapies followed in rapid succession. Periodic MRIs scanned the tumor site for signs of recurrence.

For sixteen months, Earl did well. The first suspicious MRI came near the end of 2011. Subsequent diagnostic procedures confirmed that the cancer was growing. Treatment did little to slow its progression.

During this time, Earl started coming to my house for weekly chats. We reminisced over childhood memories, laughed about long-forgotten incidents, and cried over hurts and misunderstandings. We reconnected in a way that brought us closer than we'd ever been as adult siblings.

One week, Earl confessed that he no longer believed in the Bible, or Jesus, or what we'd been taught about life after death. I listened in stunned silence, scarcely believing the words coming out of his mouth. We'd grown up in a Mennonite minister's home, attended the same church, heard the same Bible stories, listened to the same sermons. What had gone wrong?

Heaviness filled my heart as I watched Earl walk to his car that day. It wasn't just the unbelief bomb he'd dropped, but something I'd been denying for weeks was painfully obvious—he was dragging his right leg. The cancer was affecting his mobility.

I grieved for my brother's physical decline, but his spiritual condition weighed even more heavily on me. I prayed fervently that the Lord would bring him to faith before it was too late. As a nurse, I knew that the cancer could spread quickly and that it could affect his ability to think clearly.

On my daily walks, I cried out to God for my brother's salvation. "Lord," I prayed, "if I just knew that everything would turn out okay [meaning that Earl would come to faith], I'd be able to sit back and watch you at work."

Instantly, the Lord spoke within my spirit. "If you knew what was going to happen, that wouldn't require faith, would it?"

Another day, I found myself singing, "Stand still and see his glory, watch as his mysteries unfold. . . ." I had no idea how God was going to answer my prayers, but I made a deliberate decision to believe that God was at work in my brother's life.

Earl and I continued our conversations. He asked questions about my faith and listened as I shared my belief that the Bible was God's truth and that Jesus was God's son. I told him about my struggles to live a consistent Christian life. I admitted that I failed often but that God promised if I confessed my sin, he would forgive me and cleanse me from all unrighteousness.

Earl listened politely but remained mired in unbelief. I enlisted other believers to join me in intercession for Earl's salvation. I even found myself making suggestions to God on what he might do to get my brother's attention. Then the irony hit me. The One who created my brother knew exactly what it would take to bring him to faith. God didn't need my input.

Earl's condition deteriorated. He went from walking unassisted to using a cane, to being confined to a wheelchair. By late spring, he could no longer drive so I went to his house to visit. We talked about many things, but I felt a check in my spirit that prevented me from talking about his spiritual condition. Nevertheless, I had peace that God was at work in his life.

Shortly after the Fourth of July, the U.S. Independence holiday, Earl lost his remaining independence. Hospice set up a hospital bed in their living room; the nurse helped him into the bed and that's where he stayed for the next seven weeks.

By this time, Earl needed total care. He had lost the use of his right side and was rapidly losing the use of his left side. My sister-in-law and I were his caregivers. I saw Earl on a daily basis and often stayed overnight to provide respite for my sister-in-law.

One Sunday afternoon, my sister-in-law called and said that Earl was crying and asking for me. As my husband and I drove to their house, I sensed that the time had come to reopen the conversation with Earl about his spiritual condition. I prayed that God would give me his words to speak.

"I have nothing to live for," Earl said in a weak voice. "I want to die." Suffering etched deep lines in his gaunt face.

I reached for his lifeless hand and said, "May I ask you a question, Earl? I don't know when you're going to die, but whether it's now or two months from now, are you ready to meet God?"

"Yes," he said.

"Do you believe that Jesus loves you and died on the cross for your sins?"

"Yes."

"Do you believe that you will go to heaven when you die?"

"Yes."

Mixed feelings of sadness for my brother's suffering and joy at God's faithfulness collided within my spirit. We gathered around Earl's bed and prayed with him. He relaxed and fell asleep.

From that day on, my husband and I went to visit Earl each evening. We read comforting Scriptures. Psalm 23 and John 14 became favorites. At Earl's request we sang from the *Life Songs* hymnbook that we'd used in church in the 1950s and '60s. Many of those hymns speak of death and of heaven. Singing to someone who would soon experience those realities gave poignant new meaning to the old words. Most of the time, Earl listened with his eyes closed, but one evening he sang along with us, "Whiter than snow, now wash me and I shall be whiter than snow."

Before we left each evening, we gathered around Earl and prayed for God's peace to descend on the house. We asked for angels to surround his bed. We prayed that Jesus would release Earl from his ailing body and carry him home.

God answered that prayer on August 29. While I grieve deeply for the loss of my brother, I also rejoice in God's incredible grace that drew him back into the family of God.

∞

Nancy Witmer lives near Manheim, Pennsylvania. She and her husband, Dick, are the parents of two adult sons and five grandchildren. Nancy does bookkeeping for their family auto repair business. She teaches a ladies' Sunday school class at Hernley Mennonite, speaks to women's groups, and does freelance writing. Nancy enjoys reading, photography, traveling, and jewelry making.

14

Words and Deeds

Anita Hooley Yoder

∞

Growing up Mennonite, I don't remember hearing much about grace. The aspect of faith most emphasized was service. My parents modeled a life of service by being available to the many needy people around us. I attended a college with the motto "Culture for Service." After college, many of my friends (and I) chose to spend a year or more engaged in voluntary service. Faith was about what you *did* as much as what you believed or received.

To be fair, all this service was characterized as a response to God's grace and love, not something we did to earn God's favor. But the response was important. Grace was all well and good, but it better be followed up with some tangible and useful actions.

This way of orienting one's life made complete sense to me—until I started reading and writing poetry. And, perhaps more importantly, until I started reading *about* writing poetry. Strangely, it was in this context that I started learning a lot about grace.

An essay by Barbara Kingsolver contained this explanation of her creative process: "I rarely think of poetry as something I make happen; it is more accurate to say that it happens to *me*. . . . It is elementary grace, communicated from one soul to another" (*Small Wonder*, Harper Collins Publishers, 2002, 229). A seminary class introduced me to Vinita Hampton Wright, who wrote, "Creative work will demonstrate to you again and again that the world is bigger and deeper than you perceive, that God has many ways of speaking to your soul, and that the soul itself possesses much wisdom that you simply hadn't noticed before" (*The Soul that Tells a Story: Engaging Creativity with Spirituality in the Writing Life*, InterVarsity Press, 2005, 33). That sounds like grace to me.

It wasn't until college and beyond that I began to awaken to the way words can be a conduit of grace, a grace that requires no response but wonder and awe. But as I probed deeper into my love for poetry and stories and beautifully crafted essays, I realized that this love had been with me all along.

At the age of eleven or twelve, I started keeping a quote book, which I referred to in my head as "The Book." The earliest volume is filled with mostly Bible verses and popular song lyrics, sprinkled with a few of my own tentative attempts at poetry. Any time I read or heard something meaningful or interesting, something I was sure I agreed with (or something I wasn't at all sure I agreed with but still found intriguing), I copied it down in The Book.

Around the time that The Book was first being filled, I had a friend in my church youth group (I'll call him Devin) who was struggling with life, with meaning, and with faith. Devin and I would have many long conversations, in person and online, but I never quite knew what to say to him. One day, I decided to loan him The Book. "Look," I said, "I don't know if you'll find any of this helpful, but in here are a lot of things that I find meaningful and hopeful. Oh, and there's some of my own poetry, too, which is terrible— just skip those pages, please."

A couple of weeks later, Devin returned The Book to me. "Thanks," he said, looking into my eyes like he really meant it. "And I really liked your poetry."

A few years later, a friend in high school (I'll call her Shaina) was going through similar struggles. She would write me heart-wrenching notes covering three or four pages in her neat, tiny handwriting. I never knew what to write back to her. Her life was so different from mine; she faced the challenges of abuse, of poverty, and of despair. I decided that if my words couldn't help her, maybe the words of others could. I lent her The Book.

I don't remember Shaina ever telling me that The Book helped her. But I do remember her senior speech, something all of us graduating seniors were given the opportunity to do near the end of the year. In her speech, Shaina mentioned that during high school there had been several friends who she felt had literally saved her life—who had, even though they probably didn't know it, prevented her from committing suicide during her bleakest times.

Devin, the friend to whom I had first given access to my collection of deepest words, went to the same high school as we did and heard Shaina's speech. We drove home together from school that day. Pulling out of the gas station, he turned and asked me, "Was she talking about you as one of the people who helped save her life?"

"I don't know," I said, "but maybe. I think so."

"Well," he replied, "that makes two of us then."

I stared at the road ahead of us. Was he saying what I thought he was—that he, too, felt that *I* had been helpful in such a real and life-altering way?

I didn't know exactly what I had done to help Devin or Shaina. I didn't know if it was my words, the words of others I gave them, or simply my presence that had helped quell their anxious longings. Sitting in the car that afternoon, I realized that I hadn't really done anything. Something had been done through me. I hadn't set out to "serve" Devin or Shaina; I simply offered them my words, and the words of others. And, somehow, God's grace came through.

I still find that God's grace comes in words, whether I'm writing poetry or sermons or essays or Sunday school curriculum. I deeply respect others who feel called to serve in more tangible ways, to embody God's grace by teaching or nursing or cleaning up after disasters. It doesn't always, or even often, feel useful sitting by myself, copying down quotes into The Book (which is now on its fifth volume). It doesn't feel like "service" to spend hours, or even days, crafting an essay that I'm not sure anyone will even see. Yet this is the way grace comes to me, and comes through me.

The poet W. H. Auden offered a brilliant description of faithful living when he wrote, "I know nothing, except what everyone knows—if there when Grace dances, I should dance" (quoted in *Traveling Mercies: Some Thoughts on Faith*, by Anne Lamott, Random House, 1999, 138).

We are all called to witness this limber, flowing grace in ways that may or may not feel like real God-ordained service. We are called to dance and speak and write and sing. And we never know what lives we might be saving.

∞

Anita Hooley Yoder lives in Cleveland Heights, Ohio, with her husband, Ben. She is currently pursuing an MDiv degree through Bethany Theological Seminary. She is a member of Friendship Mennonite Church. She writes Sunday school curriculum for Gather 'Round *and contributes to several other publications, including* Purpose *magazine. At Goshen College, Anita studied English and secondary education and spent a summer researching new developments in Mennonite poetry. She enjoys good books, sports, poetry, ethnic restaurants, traveling, games, and time spent outdoors.*

15

Grace Changing Us

Janet Gehman

⬭

The two years I spent teaching in China included some stressful times, but one of my students became a good friend. Older than most of the students and already having some experience teaching English, Rhoda welcomed time to visit me. Led by her questions, we talked about many things, including the reason I was teaching in China. I told her I believed that God asked me to do that. When she asked questions about God, I gladly tried to answer them. It was the beginning of Rhoda's journey to a time years in the future when she could accept God's grace.

Later Rhoda wrote about that journey. "I was born in the country of no-god," she said. Although we talked about the Bible story and God's love, she secretly laughed about what she was hearing. "It sounded like a fairy tale, with no logic." Delighted, however, she read the Bible and other books I gave her "because an English teacher needs the knowledge."

The following year I moved to another college, and Rhoda returned to teach at her own school. One weekend she took a long bus ride to visit me. She seemed to be under a cloud of sadness. She went to church with me, but it impressed her "as a place that might meet the needs of old people."

After I left China, Rhoda and I stayed in touch, especially after we had email.

The next several years were quite difficult for Rhoda. Health problems, feelings of being treated unfairly in her teaching position, being single and often lonely caused a restlessness that led to a longing for peace.

One night she sat alone thinking about the future. "I found the road ahead of me narrower and narrower," she wrote. In her sadness and fear, the thought suddenly came to her that she could take early retirement. Immediately she felt relieved, even though she knew she would have less money. Her heart was lightened. "Somehow I felt that a supernatural power helped me and took me out of my trouble." Was it God? she wondered. She acted on the idea to retire early.

For some years after that, she kept debating in her mind: How could she believe in a God she could not see, but how could she doubt a power that had clearly led her to make a decision that brought her peace?

One day she received an email from a friend who had joined her husband studying in the United States. Her friend included articles about Chinese students coming to faith in God. "I read all the articles without stopping. Finally I found the answers I had been searching for," Rhoda says.

Knowing she needed a church, she dialed a number for information and found an address. That Easter morning as she sat in church and listened eagerly to the woman elder speaking, tears ran down her face. "I did not know why," she says. "Was it out of gratefulness after being mistreated, or because I had finally found the home of my soul? Yes, finally I found the amazing power that had helped me in the darkness."

When she saw new believers being baptized, she knew that she also wanted baptism. The senior pastor suggested that she wait until she understood the Bible better. "I truly felt resurrected," she says. "Although the new life was still weak and young, it had begun. And it grew each day." She was baptized on Christmas Day.

Because of health problems, Rhoda rented a house away from the city. There she found a mature church that helped lay a solid foundation of faith in God. "No matter where I would go or what changes would come in the future, I would not be away from God in whom I believed."

When she needed to move again, God led her to another small but friendly church. "I firmly believe it was the place God wanted me to go. The move was so smooth and natural. I thanked God for managing my way and accepted it gladly. There I found a team full of love. There I learned love, forgiveness, and flexibility."

Rhoda had no difficulty loving family and friends, but the Bible told her to love her enemies, those people who had made her life so hard. At first, she felt she could not obey. She had no trouble forgiving those who had unintentionally hurt her, "but I could not forgive people who hurt me intentionally again and again."

Conflict had always shaken Rhoda. She seemed unable to avoid it. Although she pretended to stay calm, she was hurt and fearful inside. But God's grace was changing her. Now she says, "Since I have a firm faith in God, I have learned love and tolerance, and all these problems have been resolved." She adds, "How beautiful it is living in the grace of God. I am thankful for God's choosing me. Also I am thankful to those who helped me grow in my life. I can enjoy God's blessing on the earth, and I will have an unimaginably happy life in heaven."

Rhoda wrote her story in 2009. In the years since then, she has found ways to continue Bible study and to be involved in various ways in her church. She says, "In return for God's grace to me, I am thinking what I should do for God. I know that whatever I do cannot compare with the salvation of God in my life."

What Rhoda may not realize is that her friendship, her letters, her story, and our prayers for each other are God's grace for me, too.

❀

Janet Gehman is a retired teacher. For more than half of her teaching years, she taught English at Lancaster Mennonite High School. She has also taught in China, Tanzania, and Lithuania. Now she does some freelance writing and editing. Her volunteer work includes working with used books at Booksavers and some adult teaching at Pathways Institute for Lifelong Learning at a local retirement home. She is a member of Hershey Mennonite Church where she teaches an adult Sunday school class. She lives in Strasburg, Pennsylvania.

16

In Christ—
The Crooked Made Straight

Eva Eberly

∞

Simona and Salvo Lombardo live in Palermo, Italy. Each shared their story with Eva Eberly. The husband, Salvo begins:

"If you aren't promoted at school this year, I'll kill you!" As a child, I believed my father would actually carry out this threat since he punished me severely when I didn't do my homework well or for other childish misdeeds. My dad grew up in a family greatly influenced by the mafia mentality in which violence is viewed as a means for gaining respect and control. He attempted to instill this lifestyle in all of us, creating an atmosphere of fear, confusion, and distrust. He often humiliated me, saying that I was a "good-for-nothing" who would never amount to anything.

Abuse in various forms was a common occurrence in our home. Consequently, I grew up having low self-esteem. I recall longing to die to escape my painful, miserable life. I thought, for what purpose do I exist anyway?

When my aunts were converted through the ministry of Mennonite missionaries, I observed the dramatic changes in their lives. At age twelve, I decided to accept Jesus into my life and intermittently attended the Shalom Mennonite Church, located in our area of Palermo. However, I remained troubled and spiritually confused. When I was sixteen, my father was incarcerated and our family broke apart. This was a time of great turmoil for all of us.

I began keeping bad company and taking drugs. The job I had pressured me into fraud and cheating, so I was on probation with the law. My life went downhill rapidly as my addictions intensified. I began living and begging on the street, throwing all self-respect, dignity, and values to the wind as I sought freedom and love. But I bitterly discovered that my heart was only growing increasingly empty and cold. One day when a street companion spit contemptuously in my face, I angrily vowed that one day I would murder him. But thankfully, God restrained me from this violent crime. Today I feel only compassion for him.

After eight years of this senseless lifestyle, I finally reached bottom and started thinking about God. His word, planted in my soul at Shalom Church, still spoke to me. A tremendous inner battle began raging. Although drawn back to church with a deep sense of guilt, I was still strongly shackled to worldly friends and vices.

During those years, the church prayed fervently for me. My pastor, Pino Arena, loved me like a father and did everything possible to help me. One night while drunk, I rang his doorbell. After he welcomed me inside, I vomited all over the house. As his wife quietly cleaned up, Pastor Arena said, "Salvo, you can't continue to live like this; you need to make a choice!"

Soon thereafter, I had a vivid dream in which God spoke to me very clearly that I needed a new birth. Kneeling beside my bed, I wept tears of true repentance and cried out to God as never before to remove my sin, "From now on, I don't care what others think. Help me to look straight ahead and keep praising you because I know that you are the only one who can save and free me!" Not only did the Lord graciously respond to the cry of my heart, but in his abounding grace, he gave me Simona, my lovely Christian wife. She has been instrumental in helping me in the struggle to break free from my painful past and to abandon my "crooked" lifestyle. Together we are rebuilding a new life of fellowship with him and others. One of the theme verses of my life is "In all your ways acknowledge him and he will make straight your paths" (Proverbs 3:6).

Simona's story. Being completely unaware of the importance of marriage in God's eyes and ignorant of God's precious teachings, my marriage at a very young age soon proved to be a tragic mistake. After escaping that trap of anguish, I began pursuing what I still hadn't found—love, understanding, acceptance, and security. But this feverish search only caused me more suffering. One after the other, I fell into the hands of those who at first seemed the "prince charming" I longed for. But every relationship left me more and more disappointed because none could fill the emptiness that grew ever greater inside me.

During that period, my sister was converted to Christ. Knowing how much I needed him, she shared the wonders Christ could do in my life. I refused to listen, thinking that following Jesus meant renouncing the attractive things I was running after. In my blindness I thought, how could a God I couldn't see meet my needs when none of the "real" people I knew and could see were able to do so? In my disillusionment, I could see no light or hope; death seemed the only way of escape. One day in my utter weariness I challenged God, "If you're a God of love, give me a way out of this labyrinth. I can't find it on my own!"

Soon thereafter, I met Emanuele, [who attended the Shalom Mennonite Church]. As we talked together, he began sharing his faith in God. This special man soon won my heart with his simplicity and awakened in me the desire to know the God that was constantly on his lips. I began realizing that God was responding to my challenge! He was opening a new chapter in my life in which I would find forgiveness for my past. Tragically, this relationship full of hopes and plans did not end as expected. Emanuele was suddenly called to be with Jesus, leaving me with greater pain than any of the past, only this time I was not alone. Jesus' presence gave me courage, strength, dignity, and meaning to that painful loss. Most of all, he gave me hope beyond death, of seeing Emanuele again, of eternity in fullness of joy and peace.

God used this grief and grace to reach the hearts of Emanuele's family. Through my witness, his mother and brothers have also opened their lives to God's grace. God reestablished my life and brought Salvo across my path, my wonderful husband with whom I share my faith and service for the Lord. Both of us have had many obstacles to overcome, but Jesus is in the midst of every battle, healing us, opening new horizons and a fresh vision of life. In God my security rests, and the empty places of my heart are filled.

∽

Simona and Salvo Lombardo are active members at Shalom Mennonite Church in Palermo, the capital city of the island of Sicily. This church is located in an area of the city that is notorious for its crime and mafia control. At every opportunity

Salvo and Simona gladly share with acquaintances and neighbors what Jesus Christ has done in their lives. They study with enthusiasm in the Discipleship Training School of the Italian Mennonite Church. Salvo assists in preaching ministry and Simona helps to lead Shalom's weekly Bible study ministry for women. Pino and Rosanna Arena are their pastors/mentors.

Adapted/translated by Eva Eberly, a long-term mission worker with Virginia Mennonite Missions who with her husband, Willard, served forty years in Italy.

Loving

17

Death, Divorce, and Deliverance

Steve Carpenter

Grace often comes in unexpected ways and from unlikely places—but it always comes exactly when it is needed most.

On a Tuesday night, September 26, 1995, the car my former wife was driving collided with an automobile operated by a woman driving under the influence of alcohol. Both Cindy, age thirty-six, and my youngest daughter, Michelle, age eleven, died that tragic night. Cindy was driving Michelle to gymnastics practice along a winding back road traversing the rolling hills of the Washington, D.C., suburbs.

Earlier that day, when the other driver left work, rather than going directly home, she stopped by a bar for happy hour in an attempt to avoid rush hour traffic. No one knows exactly how many drinks she had, since the police didn't order a blood alcohol test until the morning after the collision. Even with an allowance for wide variance in a person's ability to metabolize alcohol, it was clear in a court of law that she had been driving "under the influence" the night before when the car ahead of her slowed to turn right into a driveway. However, the impaired driver grew impatient and crossed the two solid yellow lines in the center of the road to pass, even though it was a no-passing zone. Just then, Cindy, driving a compact Ford Escort in the opposite direction, crested a hill and came directly into the path of the drunk driver's much larger vehicle.

Although Cindy and Michelle were both wearing seat belts, their car was not equipped with air bags. The resulting head-on collision killed Cindy instantly. Michelle's back was broken, and she died shortly thereafter in a nearby hospital's emergency room. The drunk driver's car did have air bags. She suffered minor injuries and was released from the hospital after several days.

I know God hates divorce and so do I. Yet, on Valentine's Day, 1989, I found myself divorced after a mere eight years of marriage to the beautiful young woman I met while stationed in Hawaii. Although we lived on separate islands, Cindy and I were in Honolulu attending the same Francis Schaeffer conference on Christian apologetics. When I first saw her she looked radiant with her long brown hair and infectious smile. Our courtship was short. Six months after meeting we were married. Two beautiful baby girls, Janelle and Michelle, came quickly thereafter. Yet all was not well in paradise. Beauty is a two-edged sword, whose fruit is sweet and alluring. After Cindy's numerous indiscretions, I could extend grace no further and filed for divorce. After a year of legal separation, our divorce was finalized. I wasn't in a hurry to jump into marriage again, so I did not date for another year. Rather, I did some serious introspection asking myself, *How had I contributed to this failed marriage?* and *What do I need to change about myself to succeed in future relationships?*

At that point, I did what many a young man has done to escape a woman: I went to sea. I requested an assignment as executive officer on the sail training ship *Eagle*, a three-masted, square-rigged sailing vessel stationed at the Coast Guard (CG) Academy in New London, Connecticut.

After two years of sailing on the *Eagle* to Europe and up and down the eastern seaboard of the United States, I was transferred to CG headquarters in Washington, D.C., an assignment I had requested in order to be closer to my daughters. It was then that I began attending Washington Community Fellowship (WCF), "an evangelical multi-denominational congregation affiliated with the Mennonite Church." It was there I met Christine Alderfer, and she became God's provision of grace for me.

Chris grew up in a Mennonite home and initially came to Washington, D.C., for a year of voluntary service as a nurse under the auspices of Mennonite Board of Missions. She was assigned to Columbia Road Health Services, which works with an underserved inner-city population. We met in 1991 in an adult Sunday school class at WCF and were married three years later on July 16, 1994. I was on active duty while we were dating and for several years after we were married. When Chris first took me home to meet her parents, they were extremely gracious. Here she was introducing her divorced, active-duty military boyfriend with two small children to her conservative, pacifist Mennonite parents. Yet, they loved and accepted me, even before I became a Mennonite pacifist, which would not happen for three more years. This was grace.

The greatest provision of God's grace, however, happened on September 26, 1995, the day of the accident, when I got the call from one of my ex-wife's neighbors to "come to the hospital. There's been an accident. And Steve, it's bad." My oldest daughter, Janelle, was thirteen years old at the time. Thankfully, she wasn't in the car that day. Rather, she was at home doing her school work. Cindy hadn't remarried, so when Cindy and Michelle died that day, Janelle was left alone. Her entire household was lost in a moment. After confirming the identities of the dead, I went to tell Janelle the sad news and to take her home to live with Chris and me.

Like most divorced men, I was a part-time Dad, bringing the girls to my townhouse on Capitol Hill on weekends. We had fun together visiting the Smithsonian museums or seeing the latest Disney movie. The first time they met Chris we took them to the circus. Chris was thirty-nine years old and had never married but loved children. I was impressed with the significant relationships she had developed with her nephews and the children of close friends. Janelle and Michelle loved her immediately. I remember the day we told them we were engaged. We took a picnic lunch and headed to Great Falls, Maryland, on the Potomac River just north of the city. They were climbing the rocky trails and admiring the rushing water when we shared our news. Their response was spontaneous and joyous.

God, in his wisdom, had provided a ready-made stepmom for Janelle—someone who could mother a grieving child and love a distraught father. Chris was God's greatest gift of grace to me and to Janelle. Without her love and support I don't think I could have made it through the darkness of the long nights that followed the accident. In the midst of Janelle's turbulent teenage years, Chris hung in with us and helped us make it through.

For her love and God's grace, I am ever thankful.

Steve Carpenter is MennoMedia's director of development. He grew up in a Presbyterian home but embraced the Mennonite faith in 1997 after a twenty-year career in the United States Coast Guard. Steve and his wife, Christine, a nurse, live in Harrisonburg, Virginia, where he served for more than eight years as Virginia Mennonite Conference coordinator. Steve is a graduate of the Coast Guard Academy, BS; Tulane University, MBA; and Eastern Mennonite Seminary, Master of Arts in religion, where his thesis explored Mennonites and Media. *Their daughter, Janelle, lives with her husband, John, in Washington, D.C.*

18

Naomi

Ruben Chupp

⌒⌒

Labor. As a pastor, today is my Sabbath. I have plans. But two sentences from Idella change everything: "Are you ready to be a grandpa? Amy's water broke." Abruptly, everything else can wait. We linger in the hallway, while daughter Amy labors with the birth of their first child. We hear it! A plaintive cry announces the birth of our first grandchild—what an amazing thing.

Birth. I ponder a grand mystery. How does love multiply in an instant? How did my affection magnify the moment Naomi Faye Kratzer was placed in my arms? Within the human soul, love surges forth in an unbounded stream from the headwaters of this sacred substance. No matter how vast the amount, there is always more. Like grace— pouring down, saturating, showering the heart, gushing, rushing, crashing, and thrashing like breakers on the shore—so comes this astonishing, startling emotion I feel for little Naomi.

"You want to hold her?" A new delight found me when this small child was gently placed in my arms. Tears of unknown but powerful origins smudged my glasses. I attended my own counsel: *breathe deep, listen closely, watch intently*. I lightly massaged tiny feet and hands. I kissed a delicate, tender cheek; drew in the soft scent of heaven. A "new" grandmother peered over my shoulder. Idella's hand caressed my arm. I couldn't stop looking at *this child*. My vision narrowed. Naomi was all I saw. Something novel and unprecedented had entered my life. So I sighed a lot, trying to inhale around something that was developing and expanding in my chest.

Becoming a grandfather has been an amazing experience. Naomi's presence in my life has surpassed all my expectations (a rare thing for me). Since her birth, I have pondered an intriguing question: How can it be that I immediately adored her so much? I wasn't introduced to her until the evening she was born. She had no being, no form, no personality. Yet when her first cry echoed in the hallway at the hospital, something happened to my heart. It was immediate. It was powerful. It was emotional. Right then and there, in that hallway, after a long wait—I loved this child! A lot. More than I could express.

Three months. When Naomi was three months old, threads of pink lint from her little booties fell onto my black pants, scattering across the dark fabric like fall leaves on a green lawn. But it didn't matter much that my pants were littered with a varnish of pink. I had been with Naomi again, had breathed in her perfume, had kissed her cheek and nuzzled her neck, had been taken in by her smile.

When I hold this small form I am astonished at how I am changed. Peace takes up more real estate in my soul. Small things remain small things, urgent agenda replaced by the importance of relationships: being with my granddaughter. When I peer into Naomi's face, I notice the image of God. God breathed spirit into her soul, imprinted divine likeness in her heart. God created Naomi's inmost essence. God has granted her the ability to think, reason, feel, choose. God has known about this lovely child from the moment of conception. She has been fearfully and wonderfully made—and she is surely the most gorgeous grandchild ever created. Except, of course, for yours.

When Naomi was born, a slumbering inner sense of familial affection was awakened. Not since the birth of my own children have I felt these emotions. Where does such love come from? I think all love comes from God. God created it, named it good.

Nine months. Now nine months old, Naomi is our little queen. When she enters the room, she commands our attention. Family adults fuss over her. She fusses back, with smiles and enough body language to make a pup appear docile. And I wonder who entertains whom?

Grandparenting is a consuming occupation. This little girl has seized our hearts, arrested our attention and turned our thoughts to mush. Naomi is a wonderment. So is our response to her. When Naomi—our gentle little queen— comes to visit, life is good—even when it isn't. She has that much power.

She is only twenty-five inches tall. She weighs about seventeen pounds. Four teeth peek through her gums. Her verbiage is limited to clicks, squeaks, coos, and laughter that chime the bells of heaven. She crawls wherever someone doesn't carry her. Awake, constant movement marks her physical carriage. And she is a little healer.

I'm a pastor. There is nothing I'd rather do. But sometimes there is too much church work and not enough of me. Pastoral leadership can be frustrating, ire becoming a companion. I slept on anger last night. At first light it was still with me. I rolled it around in cognitive gears like a kid thumbing the seams on a new baseball. I met Amy, Naomi, and Idella to celebrate Idella's birthday. Wife, daughter, and daughter's daughter celebrated Grandma's birthday at KFC.

I held Naomi close. She held *me* close. While her momma
and grandma talked, Naomi and I went outside. Naomi
intently examined the leaves on a tree, totally engrossed.
She laid her head on my shoulder, caressed the back of my
neck with a stray hand. I listened to her breathe. I drew in
her aroma. I nuzzled her cheek. I loved her without conditions. She loved me the same way.

Returning to the restaurant, I sat with Naomi on my
lap while she chewed the edge of a Pepsi glass. My anger
was gone, anxiety dissipated. Redemption had occurred.
Shalom visited me in those moments with this little child.
The rule of God seemed within reach. Emotional redemption, authored by this Little One, had silenced my unholy
unction from the night before. All was right with the world
again. My healer was the littlest member of the family:
diminutive Naomi Faye Kratzer.

∞

A Prayer for Naomi. *God, you have known my Naomi
from conception: creating her inmost being, knitting her
together in her mother's womb. Her tiny frame was not
hidden from you in that secret place. Look after Naomi
all the days of her life. Help her grow up big and strong.
Knead into her soul the essence of Jesus. Grant my first
grandchild the wisdom to know the ways and will of the
Christ. May she follow him all the days of her life. Thank
you, God, for letting me hold the next generation. I am
rendered speechless by the holy power of my moments with
this Little One. She is grace to me. I am grateful. Amen.*

∞

*Ruben Chupp is a follower of Jesus, husband, father,
grandfather (of nine Little Ones, ages four through nine),*

Mennonite pastor (for twenty-three years), convinced Anabaptist, and an observer of the world around him. There have been many significant and important transitions in his life, but the easiest one was becoming a grandfather. His grandchildren have taught him much about things like acceptance, grace, and unconditional love. His passions include reading, writing, photography, and traveling. But mostly, when he can do anything he wants to, he hangs out with his grandchildren, playing UNO, reading with them, listening carefully, regarding life through their eyes.

19

Grace through Adoption and Emigration

Lovella Schellenberg

∽

I've often wondered if my grandmother Helena Klassen, who was expecting her thirteenth child during a time of a revolution, worried about what would happen to the baby she was carrying. She had no other option but to trust God's grace for the little one as she herself died while he was yet an infant.

That son, Aron, was born in the Mennonite village of Suworovka, Orenburg, Russia, in 1918, a year after the Bolsheviks had overthrown the czar's government. The village struggled to survive, and by 1920 the few seeds that they managed to hide from marauding robbers failed to grow because the rain they desperately needed did not come.

In the same village, God was stirring the heart of a well-established young couple who had married in 1911 and did not have any children of their own. They approached my grandfather asking if he would consider allowing the little toddler to become their own. Though Aron was young, he retained a faint memory of being carried by a young girl to the home of Bernhard and Katherina Peters. He had a small green velvet purse as a keepsake from his mother, and though family attempts to visit Aron continued, it became necessary for them to end because of the tearful goodbyes. Aron was joined at the Peters home by another adopted child called Eleanor, and the new family did their best to make a life in Russia even as the conditions continued to erode. Bernhard and Katherina courageously decided to take their little family to Canada. They beseeched other family members to come with them, but the rest chose not to go, fearing the unknown more than the known.

Packing enough clothes for travel, a few photos, and a blueprint from the estate they walked away from, the four said goodbye to their loved ones, knowing they might never see them again. Making their way to Moscow, they were delayed when the children became seriously ill with measles. Staying in a strange city that seemed full of evil intent, they feared for their safety and wondered if they had chosen a road too difficult. Finally, consent was given for them to travel to England where they were required to pass final inspection before boarding the ship to Canada. Aron, who was shy, refused to speak. His mental capacity was questioned, and at first he was declared to be mute. His father was excused, and several kind, Low German-speaking officials took little Aron and coaxed him into speaking by asking him which games he liked to play with his sister.

They boarded the vessel *Montcalm*, went to the lower decks, and after weeks of seeing nothing but water arrived in St. John, New Brunswick, on March 22, 1925. Though they felt alone and arrived with very little in terms of earthly possessions, my grandparents made it clear that they were humbled by the grace of God, free from communism and once again able to worship without fear of reprisals.

Settling in the community of Waldheim, Saskatchewan, they were given shelter on the property of another

Mennonite family where the family of four slept crosswise on one bed. Understanding not one word of English, Aron and Eleanor were sent to school with a piece of brown paper that was recycled from a dry goods purchase at the local general store. If the language barrier and the visible poverty was not daunting enough, they also soon realized that the clothing they wore marked them at once as being *Rüsslanders.*

With a fierce determination to succeed, my grandfather found work clearing land and chopping wood. This difficult work was harder than anything he had done on their estate in Russia, but knowing there was no other way to survive, my grandfather repeated over and over, "I have to, I have to, there is no other way!"

Though my dad, Aron, occasionally talked about the difficulties of those early years, he never neglected to describe to us how grateful they were for God's grace that they were able to leave communism to live in a land of freedom. His formal education ended in order to work with his father while he was a young teen. Yet in his seventies, he painstakingly wrote his life story by hand so that we might have a record of his life. Realizing that putting on paper what he had experienced in life would not come naturally, he began by writing, "May God give me grace to write how he led me in my life that it may not be an offence but a blessing to others."

He was thankful for the fact that he had three mothers in his life. His first mother gave birth to him, one raised him, and one became his stepmother later in life. It was, he said, similar to the idea that he was adopted three times. He was first adopted by Bernhard and Katherina Peters; later he was adopted as a son-in-law when he married, but it was the third adoption that he considered the most significant. He was adopted into the family of God when he accepted Christ as his Savior.

Seven decades after he last saw his siblings, my parents traveled to Europe. Upon mentioning to the flight attendant that he was going to be reunited with his family, she arranged to have my dad see the sunrise from the cockpit. He stood in wonder at the brilliant red sky before him and marveled that he was about to be a part of a wonderful reunion: three remaining children out of thirteen reuniting after seventy years. "God's great love has made this possible," said my dad.

As they drove up the street to his sister's home, they saw an elderly woman wearing a kerchief, dressed in her Sunday best. Without words they embraced and clung to one another; later the scene was repeated when his brother enveloped him and with a quivering voice said, "*Mine liebster bruder*" (My dearest brother).

Dad was an unassuming man who humbly approached God's throne of grace. Amazed at the grace bestowed on him by others, he would have a certain look that reflected surprise at each act of kindness showed to him. His mother died when he was an infant, his father died of starvation, he was taken to live with strangers, and yet he always gave me the impression that he was given undeserved grace. As he lay in his hospital bed waiting to be called home at eighty-one years of age, I held his hand and watched his breathing slow and his spirit shift from one life of grace to the next.

∞

Lovella Schellenberg lives in Abbotsford, British Columbia, on a chicken farm with her husband, Terry. They are blessed to have two sons, two daughters-in-law, and five precious grandchildren. She founded the Mennonite Girls Can Cook *blog in 2008 and has coauthored two cookbooks, the newest of which is* Mennonite Girls Can Cook Celebrations, *published in 2013.*

20

Just the Right Thing

Joanne Klassen

∞

Ask, and it will be given . . . (Matthew 7:7, NIV)

When we were growing up, he was my pesky younger brother. As teenagers we had very different interests and separate circles of friends. As adults my younger brother and I had drifted away from each other with each passing decade. We lived nearly a thousand miles apart—me in Winnipeg, Manitoba, and Don in Edmonton, Alberta. Each of our lives overflowed with career, community, and family responsibilities. We'd last seen one another on two unscheduled trips to Michigan to attend the funerals of our parents. Dad died in February and Mom a little over a month later. Both Don and I were enveloped in grief; these visits flew by in a blur.

Later I was pleased to be asked to lead a writing workshop in Edmonton and called Don to see if I could visit him and his wife for a few days when my work was complete.

The warm welcome I received was heartwarming. It included wonderful home-cooked meals, blazing fires each day, walks to a nearby lake with their dogs, and conversation that reached backward and forward in time, the kind of conversation only people who have occupied space in one another's lives since childhood can enjoy. My stay turned out to be a much-needed personal retreat. I hadn't been in their home in years and our time together left me with a lot to think about and give thanks for.

Don is a social worker in a one thousand-bed inner-city hospital. At sixty-five years old and quite a bit over six feet tall, with a sturdy Scandinavian build, he's a person that people look up to for more reasons than one. The path to his profession has been anything but smooth. He has known personal challenges and family tragedy that can make or break a person. Don's calm, reassuring manner was born of finding a path through some of the worst things life can throw at a person and finding a way out the other side, ready to help others navigate the cliffs in their personal journeys.

A promising football player in his teens, my brother broke all ten fingers in an early season game that ended his playing for good. He married soon after high school and became a father, then a single father of two. He delivered mail for a dozen years in Michigan before moving to Canada and becoming a journeyman electrician working for the railway. Years of punishing outdoor work took their toll. At forty, Don received a disability pension and had to learn to live with nearly debilitating daily back pain. After much soul searching, he entered university and completed a degree in social work. Don worked in a variety of settings, eventually moving to Alberta where he lives today.

Don is often called upon to mentor less-experienced social workers, either formally or informally. Death is something he has witnessed many times and he is able to bring a confident presence to people who are facing death, as well as to families experiencing the grief of the approaching death of a loved one.

One young colleague at the hospital where Don works told me, "It seems that Don knows exactly what to do and say, which is different in each situation."

Puzzled, I asked Don, "How *do* you always know what is just the right thing?"

Don told me what he tells others: "I ask. For example, if someone has not had many visitors, I ask, 'Would you like some company or would you prefer to be alone?' Sometimes they cannot speak, but they lift a finger or nod. I may ask, 'Would you like me to hold your hand?'"

Don was determined to learn as much as possible about the traditions and practices of the cultures that he encounters so that he can offer what might be comforting, but he never assumes to know what might be wanted. He told me of a large family that gathered around the bed of a dying relative. As they waited for a priest to arrive, he asked what he might do for them. They asked him to pray. Theirs was not his religious tradition, but he knew from experience the words of comfort spoken in their faith and offered a prayer with confidence. They looked at him with amazement and expressed gratitude.

It was no coincidence that I had the opportunity to have these conversations about death with Don. I had attended three funerals in as many months. The night before I left for my trip to Edmonton a dear friend, Bill, died. I pondered at length how to approach Carol, Bill's wife, when my husband and I went to visit her on my return home. I wondered, like Don's fellow social workers, what the right thing was to say or do for Carol, the one left behind. From Don's lead I was able to phone Carol and ask what would be just right for her by way of support. We'd planned to visit her; she mentioned phone calls as a way she preferred to have friends reach out. I am so glad I asked.

Returning home, I carry with me the gift of my younger brother's wisdom and his words: "Ask." I thank God for the grace of placing my brother Don in my path—it was just the right thing at the right time. This is what I have come to recognize as God's signature.

∞

Joanne Klassen moved to Winnipeg, Manitoba, from Ann Arbor, Michigan, to help found The Centre for Human Development. Her first book, Learning to Live, Learning to Love *(Jalmar Press, 1985), was translated into Greek and Russian. She has written many books and contributes to numerous periodicals. In 1998 Joanne had a vision to create Heartspace Writing School, using Transformative Writing™ as a path to wholeness through reflective personal writing. She teaches Transformative Writing at Woodbrooke Quaker Study Centre in Birmingham, England, and Canadian Mennonite University in Winnipeg. She is cofounder of the European Centre for Life Writing for Transformation.*

21

Love Multiplied through Grace

Ruth Smith Meyer

⬯

I could hardly believe it that April day—it was my fifth birthday of sitting alone, celebrating the life of my husband, and remembering. Gathering the letters and cards he had given me over the years, I snuggled down in my leather recliner. For almost an hour I read and felt again his love for me. One reminded me of a conversation we had a few nights before he died.

"Ruth," he whispered, "I want you to know that I hope you get married again when I am gone."

"Oh, Norman!" I protested.

"I know you don't want to hear it now, but when you meet the right man and feel love again, I want you to know that I would approve. You have given me so much and you still have love to give. I hope you can find someone who can benefit from life with you."

I leaned back on my chair, sighed, and spoke aloud, "Norman, I don't think that is going to happen, but it's okay. I'm learning to live life alone. I'm finding other things to fill my life."

Lifting my face, I prayed, "But God, if this is your plan, please don't make my life too long."

At that moment the phone rang. Allowing myself one more quick sigh, I answered, "Hello?"

"Hi! This is Paul Meyer."

Paul Meyer! We had grown up less than a mile apart, swam in the same swimming spot in the summer, and shared toboggan rides on the hills between our homes. We had visited each other as young marrieds. Norman admired Paul, for they had a lot in common. Later, we both moved in different directions and lost touch.

When Paul's wife died, I didn't hear about it until after the funeral, so I sent a card and small note to convey my condolences. As I did with anyone who had lost a spouse, I included my telephone number in case the bereaved wanted to talk to someone who understood. Now, a year later, he called. He had been going through the sympathy cards received after Marion's death and came across my note.

Two hours later we concluded the call, warmed and sweetly gratified with a pleasant time of catching up and reminiscing about common acquaintances. I had always thought Paul a quiet man and was amazed with what ease and comfort we communicated. As I thought about our conversation, I felt as though God was smiling down at me.

"Whoa here, God!" I protested, "He just called to thank me for my note—that's all!"

But I only felt God smile more.

A few more telephone calls and an afternoon visit confirmed what we both had been feeling—there was a real sense of comfort and companionship with each other.

We began to regularly see each other. Each time, the comfort deepened and love grew. By that time there was no doubt in my mind that God was giving us a gift only he in his grace could have planned.

Later, I shared with Paul the prayer I was voicing when his first call came. His eyes twinkled and a grin spread across his face.

"Wait until I tell you the rest of the story!"

"The rest of the story?"

"That evening it took a while to have the courage to call. In fact I dialed your number four or five times before I had the nerve to let it ring at your end." He paused. "I think I needed to wait until you prayed that prayer."

With this revelation, Paul and I knew God was bringing us together. We felt enveloped in God's goodness and grace.

He told me that he was on call for knee surgery in the coming year, and I was glad I could be there for him. Six weeks before our wedding, at an annual check-up, Paul's family doctor recommended seeing a specialist because his PSA (Prostate-specific antigen) was slightly elevated. He assured Paul it wasn't a serious concern but nonetheless advisable. The specialist had the same reaction but scheduled a biopsy to certify everything was all right.

"Should we postpone the wedding until we know whether I have cancer?" Paul asked.

"I'm sorry, Paul, but it's too late for that. I already love you deeply and would rather go through it with you than to have you face it alone if it should prove to be cancer."

Two weeks after our quiet December wedding, we went to get the results of the biopsy.

"It's not good news," the doctor said with a grim expression, "All twelve samples were malignant, ten a very aggressive type of cancer. There is no alternative; you need surgery as soon as possible."

I could have panicked, but I had a strong sense that I was right where God wanted me to be and was overwhelmed with a feeling of joy in having the privilege of sharing Paul's life even if it might be only a short while.

The surgery in February went well. In April, he had his first knee replacement. We had a lovely summer as he recuperated. In September and October he had thirty-three radiation treatments. It was only the last few that caused some blistering. Although it surprised us, his second knee replacement was scheduled for November. Immediately afterward he complained of a stretching feeling between his hip and knee. The following May, he experienced drop foot, probably caused by his epidural. That necessitated a brace.

The seven years since our marriage have held prolonged periods of intense pain for Paul, weakening of his muscles on the left side, and many physiotherapy sessions. This year after finding tumors inside his spine, he had unsuccessful back surgery, five radiation treatments, and a series of chemo.

Many have expressed their sympathy and concern over the tragic turn in our lives since our marriage. But to us, we've felt God's grace in many ways: miracles when pain was relieved for months at a time; the overwhelming support of our family, churches, and friends; the intense and abiding joy we find in each other; abundant grace for each day as we need it; and above all, the sure belief that we are exactly where God planned us to be and that he is directing each step of our way. We've found with hymnwriter Annie Johnson that "To added afflictions He adds His mercy; to multiplied trials He multiplies peace." What an exciting discovery!

∞

Ruth Smith Meyer is a member of The Word Guild, Canada's largest Christian writers' guild, and Inscribe Christian Writers Fellowship. She is a regular contributor to the daily devotional Rejoice!, *the author of two adult novels and a children's book, and a contributor to the widely acclaimed anthologies* Second Cup of Hot Apple Cider *and* Grandmothers' Necklace. *Her articles have appeared in a variety of magazines, and her inspirational speaking has taken her to many areas of Ontario and the U.S. She and her husband, Paul Meyer, divide their time between Listowel and Ailsa Craig, Ontario, to stay in touch with their families. Website: www.ruthsmithmeyer.com.*

Pain

22

Extreme Forgiveness

Interview with John Perkins

∞

In the late '60s, some of us staged an economic boycott in Mendenhall, Mississippi, and were locked in jail there. Students from nearby colleges would come on a Saturday and participate in the boycott. On our way back home after the demonstration, we would have a march. We would have some speech making and say we were going to hold out until they changed the way they treated black people in our town.

But the Brandon Jail incident happened in 1970 and was a different story. One day nineteen people were arrested and put in the Brandon jail. We needed to make bond for them to get them out of jail, so we went to the jailhouse. The jailhouse was surrounded by highway patrols. Someone went to the sheriff and told him that we were there to make bond. The sheriff could hardly believe we would actually come to the jail—to make bond. Now that I look back, I didn't have any understanding of the hostility that these people had.

And so they started beating three of us before we got into the jail. Once we got inside, the sheriff began to curse us and say, "This is that smart nigger. This is a new ballgame, now. This is not Mendenhall. You in my county now." They began to beat and torture us and the rest of it is just a horror story.

We were stamped on and the horrible thing is that one of the sheriffs took a pistol and cocked it and put it aside my head and pulled the trigger. Well, of course there wasn't a bullet. It didn't go off, but in my mind, I was a dead person. That was part of the [torture]. They wanted to destroy me and they all wanted to kick me in my groin. It was like I was some kind of a negative sex object, that they wanted to destroy this Negro, black, sex object. I think it came out unconsciously in many ways; it came out in the way they handled prisoners.

In jail I saw a racial hatred in their eyes that frightened me—that people could possess that. I was afraid that might become a part of my life and so I said, "This is a dark place and I don't want that dark place in my own life." I made a commitment in jail that night. I realize that I was bargaining with God, so I'm not playing a hero role. I was fearful. I was thinking I was going to be killed. And I was making a bargain with God. I said, "God, if you'll let me out of this jail, I really want to preach a gospel that is stronger than my race, stronger than any economic interest. I want to preach a gospel that can reconcile not only blacks and whites, but black and whites together in the body of Christ." That's what keeps me going.

I'm probably one of the first people who experienced that kind of beating around the time [of the boycotts] and I really believe that in telling my story even right after I was out of prison, they could see that my head and eyes were swollen and all of that. I think the general Mississippi public knew that something had happened. And they believed our story because of the calmness of it. It was almost undeniable. I think if I would have been shouting into the microphone, they would have said, he deserved that. That's why they beat him. You know, he deserved it.

Then I became friends with a local (different) sheriff. Sometimes you meet somebody and your chemistry just jives. I'm sort of a competitive person and he was just as competitive as I am and so we sort of hit it off. He started telling me about the failure of the prison system and that he has such a concern of how can we come up with something that can rehabilitate these young people. And he said, "Many of them shouldn't be in these prisons for these long periods." And he said that many churches and organizations come into the prison and have religious worship with them, and that's okay and good, but the big problem is that when they go out, 80 percent of them come back. "So it's on the outside we need all this care for these people," he said. "We need this nurture for them out there." He started talking to me about the idea of, why don't we get together and try to organize some churches to work with kids both on the inside and on the outside.

So I'm really, really excited about the [reconciliation] ministry that we have established here in Jackson. It's not so much for the sheriff who tortured me—my reconciliation is not so much toward the white people. It is really grace for me. You know I was able to see the burden, the anguish, the hatred in the eyes of the people that were torturing me in that jail. That hate scared me.

I'm doing what I'm doing—yes—in obedience to God, but there is a joy and a freeing spirit that comes from that kind of obedience. There's a sense of gratitude to God. The joy of the Lord is my strength.

∞

John M. Perkins grew up in New Hebron, Mississippi, the son of a sharecropper. After his older brother's murder at the hands of a town marshal, John fled to California, vowing never to return. However, after converting to Christianity in 1960, he returned to Mendenhall, Mississippi, to share the gospel of Christ. While in Mississippi, his outspoken nature and support and leadership in civil rights demonstrations resulted in repeated harassment, beatings, and imprisonment. Perkins is the founder of the John M. Perkins Foundation for Reconciliation and Development and author of the classic Let Justice Roll Down *and, more recently,* Leadership Revolution: Developing the Vision & Practice of Freedom & Justice *(Regal Books, 2012) and* Love Is the Final Fight: A Memoir *(Regal Books, 2011).*

Interviewed by Jerry L. Holsopple, producer for Journey Toward Forgiveness, *a documentary produced by Mennonite Media in 2001.*

23

The Pit of Destruction

Sena Friesen Meilleur

∞

What are you doing here and who gave you permission to cut out a grave for yourself here, hewing your grave on the height and chiseling your resting place in the rock? (Isaiah 22:16 NIV)

A Little League game is going on in the neighborhood park. I find myself sitting in the stands, watching dully as the kids swing bats and throw balls and run and run. I sit with my forearms on my knees, a brick in my stomach, watching and listening as the shrieks and shouts of the children drift away into the blue summer sky.

It is time to move on. I wander down the street, then sit under a tree for awhile, just wanting to sink into sleep, wishing the roots of the tree would ease apart and let me down into the cool soil, down, down into the earth where I could finally rest.

I get up and walk on. My feet are leading me home. But as I turn onto my street, I see my husband's car in the driveway of our house; I turn on my heel and keep walking.

Two days later I sit in the office of Leora Black, PhD, licensed marriage and family therapist. Speechless with sobs I choke out the words.

I can't stay married anymore.

That's about all I can manage for that session; then it's home to the house my husband and I had bought with so much excitement several years before, when we'd been so happy.

The next week, back in Dr. Black's office, I sit and weep some more. Finally one day I tell her my plan: turning my car on in the closed garage and falling asleep.

She doesn't even seem shocked. That's one thing I love about Dr. Black. Nothing ever seems to shock her: not my shameful admission about my failed marriage and not my plan to die. She simply leans forward in her chair and says gently, "Sena, there is another option."

"No." I shake my head dully, looking at my wedding ring. "I can stay married, or I can die. Since I can't stay married anymore, I don't want to keep living."

"Stay married . . . or die." She lets the silence hang in the air for a moment. "There is a third choice, you know."

"No," I say again. "I don't believe in divorce."

She leans back in her chair and shrugs almost impercept-ibly. Once again she lets the silence linger, as a sob shivers in my chest. I say again, "I don't believe in divorce."

"So you would rather *die?*" she says. "Do you really feel that is what God wants for you?"

"I don't know what God wants," I say miserably. "God hasn't spoken to me in years."

"Forget about God, then," she says, almost impatiently. "The world—the universe—the human race. How is any-one helped by you carrying out your plan? Your family? Your sister? Your mother?"

The sob comes shuddering out. I think of my dear sister's face. She had said to me once: "Sena, if you killed yourself, you would take me with you." She had pulled me back from the edge of the abyss once; maybe again the thought of her will be enough to save me.

Leora's words whisper in the chambers of my brain: *There is a third option.*

∞

And so somehow I find myself divorced. My heart feels like a broken stone in my chest. I feel crushed at times by overwhelming guilt.

A couple of years go by. Things are looking up. I have bought a little condo, and I have a dog, and I'm dating a nice man. The man persuades me to go to church again, and slowly, day by day, I begin to breathe again.

But I still find myself haunted by my marriage and divorce and my grief. These thoughts come to me often while walking my dog, Bandit. There is something about poking along behind a dog who insists on sniffing every blade of grass and every pebble that leads one's mind to wander.

One summer night while walking with Bandit, my thoughts turn again to my feelings of grief and guilt. I wonder how long I will feel this way, if it will ever get better. I know what I need to do; I need to forgive myself. But I'm not sure I know how.

The air is warm and still; a bird whispers in the darkness over my head and the streetlight casts a pool of light on the sidewalk. Bandit trots into the light and stops to sniff the air, then carries on.

I keep thinking about forgiveness. I have long since forgiven my former husband for his role in our divorce, but I can't seem to forgive myself. A voice in my mind says I'm not worthy of forgiveness.

I stop while Bandit investigates a dead leaf. Is it true? I'm not worthy of forgiveness? I draw a breath of the night air and ask in the night: Does God forgive me?

Yes.

The answer is there in my heart instantly, and so clearly I know it hadn't come from me. My own thoughts are never so clear.

Yes, you are forgiven and loved.

So loved I can't even comprehend it!

It's been so long since I have prayed, I don't really know what to do. I stand in the darkness, listening to Bandit snort in a tuft of grass while a warm breeze stirs my hair. I just stand and allow myself to feel loved. I don't have any answer.

And then as the forgiveness and love seep into my bones, I feel gripped with joy as I realize what has just happened: God spoke to me! To me! Standing on a sidewalk, under a streetlight with a bag of dog poop in one hand . . . God spoke to me! I feel like celebrating, like shouting and laughing and crying all at once.

Instead, I turn for home, calling to Bandit, who trots up to join me as we go inside. With a full heart I lock the door and turn off the porch light, knowing I will hear God's voice again.

> *Surely it was for my benefit that I suffered such anguish. In your love you kept me from the pit of destruction; you have put all my sins behind your back. (Isaiah 38:17 NIV)*

Sena Friesen Meilleur lives in Essex Junction, Vermont, with her husband, Kevin, and dogs, Bandit and Gus. Sena and Kevin are members of First Congregational Church of Essex Junction. Sena graduated from Union Institute and University in 2004. She works as a registered employee benefits consultant and is a writer and artist. Her writing has appeared in numerous periodicals, including With Magazine, Guideposts for Teens, Purpose, Discovery *and* Teen Life. *Sena is a recipient of the Evangelical Press Association's Higher Goals in Christian Journalism Award (1998).*

24

The Labor Pains of Love

Gordon Houser

∞

In 1985, a year I described at the time as my worst ever, I also discovered the strange power of God's grace coming to me in a way I would never have chosen. In fact, I bitterly opposed it.

I was married to Jeanne and father to Ethan, who was two-and-a-half. Jeanne and I wanted a second child. We'd already had two miscarriages in the previous year and were expecting again. Jeanne was nearly twelve weeks along, and we were hoping to hear a heartbeat at our next appointment with the obstetric/gynecology doctor. Then Jeanne had some bleeding. We each prayed, and each of us felt the Lord saying the baby would be okay.

Our church encouraged the practice of "listening to the Lord," which is a concentrated way of praying that involves imagining the Lord (Jesus, the Spirit, however one might image God's voice) giving a person a message. It's not an audible voice but a sense. The church encouraged this practice but also emphasized the need to discern with others whether or not a message was really "from the Lord."

Jeanne and I each had a sense of the Lord assuring us the baby was fine. As it turned out, however, the baby was already dead. We went to the doctor and learned that the fetus had stopped growing at about eight weeks. On the way home from the doctor's office, I leaned out the car window and yelled to the sky, "You bastard!"

I understand this may sound silly to some and blasphemous to others—silly because, obviously, God didn't cause the baby to die, and blasphemous because you just don't address God that way. But my shout was not from some rational side of me but from my heart, my gut. It was a cry of anguish and anger, of feeling loss and feeling betrayed. At that point I experienced a loss of faith—in my own ability to hear God's voice and in the God I prayed to.

As I was to discover later, I did not lose my faith in God but in the image of God I carried within me. And I still believed enough to yell at him.

I stopped praying. What's the use, I thought. God didn't answer my most heartfelt prayer. Why pray at all? It seemed false, merely going through motions, dishonest. I told my small group and others in church what I felt. They didn't judge me but said, "We will have faith for you." One of the most meaningful responses for me came from my close friend, Vicki, who does not normally use "colorful" language. When she heard the news of the miscarriage, she said, "Shit!" At that moment I felt such empathy from her. I knew she understood. And I felt relief that my crisis of faith was not going to bring others down. This gave me freedom to experience it fully.

The next few months were dark. I fell into a depression, though I was able to continue my job. Still, I was a lousy husband, offering little support to Jeanne, who was dealing with her own grief.

Outside the support of our church, two things helped turn me around. One was a letter from Richard Rohr, a

Catholic priest with whom I'd stayed a couple of days in 1977, when he was a leader at New Jerusalem Community in Cincinnati. Later he founded the Center for Action and Contemplation in Albuquerque, New Mexico. We had corresponded occasionally, and I saw him a couple of times when he was leading retreats. During that fall of 1985, I wrote him and described my loss of faith. On October 2, he wrote me one of the most beautiful letters I've ever received. Full of empathy and affirmation, the letter said that God was inviting me to "a deeper Center, . . . your true Center where you are grounded in the Absolute, where *you and He are already One* and already deeply in love [his emphasis]." Richard wrote that I was "created for Absurd Love. The space for it is growing inside you now." He did not promise comfort but said, "The labor pains of Love will probably be long and very real. . . . It is yours to bear."

All I felt was pain, yet Richard said this was part of a process that would actually draw me closer to God, who was not some servant to do my bidding or a fickle tyrant, but a Father who created me for Absurd love. The letter lit in me a spark of hope.

A week before I received Richard's letter, I attended a retreat at the Manna House of Prayer in Concordia, Kansas, led by James Finley, a contemplative writer who was a novice under Thomas Merton in the 1960s at the Trappist monastery Gethsemani. He spoke of God as "the Really Real," who is infinitely present, loving mercy. I spoke with Finley about my inability to pray the prayer of petition (asking God for something). He said we can't make God more present, caring, or merciful by asking, but we may increase our awareness of that care and mercy.

This was helpful, but prayer still seemed too much a fiction. It made no sense to me. For months, all I could pray each day was Psalm 62:1b: "For God alone my soul waits in silence." Everything else seemed false.

Eventually I came to a place of praying for others, even myself, but I did so without any expectation that these prayers would effect a change. I'd learned (whether true or not) that I had no control over what God might do. Yet I'd come to believe that I should be honest in my prayers—tell God what I wanted, confess my shortcomings, express my thanks, and acknowledge my dependence on God for my very breath.

A second element of grace came from a doctor we saw who specialized in genetics. His baldly rational, scientific approach was oddly comforting. He explained that a miscarriage occurs because something is wrong with the fetus and that this occurs in about a quarter of pregnancies and often goes undetected. He also advised waiting until after the miscarried fetus would have been born before trying to get pregnant again.

A year and eight months after the miscarriage that sent my faith into a tailspin, our daughter Abri was born. Yet another sign of grace.

∞

Gordon Houser is a long-time Mennonite journalist and church member. He is the author of Present Tense: A Mennonite Spirituality *(Cascadia),* Relatively Speaking: Strengthening Families Ties, *and contributed to* Wrestling with God: Devotions for Men. *He serves as associate editor of* The Mennonite, *the magazine of Mennonite Church USA. He is a member of New Creation Fellowship Church, a Mennonite congregation in Newton, Kansas. Houser is married to Jeanne, and they have two children, both married.*

25

Dancing in the Rain

John Eby

∞

*"Life is not waiting for the storm to pass, but learning
to dance in the rain."—attributed to Vivian Greene*

For the last two years I read the above statement nearly
every day, many days several times. It is posted on our
kitchen cabinet, "Photoshopped" on a photo I took one
evening of the sun peeking through menacing clouds. I also
read it on a plaque as we left the office of our oncologist
in January 2011 when our comfortable life was shattered
with the report that the discomfort my wife, Joyce, felt in
her abdomen was stage three small cell neuroendocrine
cancer, very rare in that location, and terminal.

For reasons I do not understand and do not accept will-
ingly, God does not prevent storms or even make them go
away. Bad things like cancer happen to good people. Over
the past two years I have experienced the grace of God in
the storm through the love and care of family and friends,

particularly our church family, and through opportunities that seemed to need God's special intervention to happen.

Joyce had an amazing tenacity and determination to live as normally as possible. Even the frequent drives to and from chemo treatment became times for meaningful conversation. Fortunately the surgeries and chemo treatments were not as disabling for her as for some. When she spent most of the day sleeping on her lounge chair exhausted from the effects of chemo, she still kept up her involvement in Bridge of Hope (a ministry helping single mothers achieve independence) by attending board and committee meetings, selling fundraising coupon books, and driving a woman to and from work and helping her get her license and a donated car so she could drive herself.

Our church community and care group were vehicles of God's grace. Joyce did not miss Sunday worship, Wednesday Night Out, the monthly meetings of the church board, the Friday Women's Fellowship, nor the monthly meetings of the book group she started. In a way her strong will "made" grace happen.

Joyce figured out a way for our family to do something together nearly every week and periodically arranged for a lunch or breakfast of her local Rutt siblings. During soccer season we attended games of three of our grandsons. The weather at the last game was cold and rainy, yet she insisted on sitting on the sidelines bundled up with several layers of clothes and covered with a wool blanket.

Several months after her diagnosis, as a fifth grade writing assignment to nominate a "person of the year," two of our grandsons wrote tributes to Joyce. Those two tributes identifying her as generous, optimistic, hardworking, and selfless from ten-year-old boys still hang on our refrigerator door as gifts of grace.

As a diversion from study while I was in graduate school more than forty years ago, we learned to ski. It became a special thing we could do together. For many years we took a ski trip to Utah with two of Joyce's brothers. Of course, cancer intruded into the decision of whether or not we could go in 2012, but we went. Until she died, Joyce bragged that she could keep up with the rest of us for a whole day, all week. Her doctor proudly displays a picture of her on the ski slope in the room where patients receive chemo.

One of the things on our bucket list was a trip to Alaska. When it became clear that her health was declining, we identified a window of about three weeks in August between other commitments when we could go. Several agents told us that it would be impossible to find a tour with such short notice, but one found the exact land and cruise tour that we preferred. The relaxed time on the cruise gave us opportunity to celebrate our rich life together and the fiftieth wedding anniversary we would not celebrate the following June.

One of the many highlights of that trip was seeing Mt. McKinley on a beautiful clear day. Our guide said it was the best view he had seen that season. Most of the trip from there on was rainy, but Alaska has special beauty in the rain. We talked about the paradox of seeing the power of God in creating such a majestic and grand mountain while we were facing cancer. We used a picture of Mt. McKinley on the cover of the bulletin for her memorial service.

At the fall 2011 benefit auction of Lancaster Mennonite School, one of the more unusual auction items was a hot air balloon ride. I was not aware, but Joyce had dreamed of taking a balloon ride, so we bought it. After several cancellations because of weather, our ride was scheduled for election day, November 2012. Because our grandsons had the day off from school, the whole family was able to come to see us off and meet us when we landed. When we arrived, the operator offered us four tickets at half price because of a cancellation. It was an unexpected gift of grace that circumstances, even cancellations, came together so that we could share the thrill of a hot air balloon ride on a sunny day over Lancaster County with our four grandsons just eighteen days before Joyce died.

The night before Joyce died, the Saturday after Thanksgiving, after hearing that the last medical procedure had failed, God was present in a particularly wonderful way. Joyce was alert. Our whole family was able to be with her in the hospital. We sang and prayed and reminisced. Our oldest grandson played the hauntingly beautiful *Ashokan Farewell* on his violin. It was a real gift of grace for each of us to say goodbye in our own way and together. After a night of rest she died peacefully. Since it was a holiday, the hospital was not busy. Our whole family and several of her siblings spent several hours together before her body was taken so her corneas could give another person sight.

While the storm did not go away, through the gift of God's grace, we "danced in the rain!"

∞

John W. Eby is a retired professor of sociology from Messiah College who lives in Dillsburg, Pennsylvania. He and Joyce served in many church-related administrative, teaching, board member, and service roles. John attends the Slate Hill Mennonite Church in Camp Hill, Pennsylvania.

26

A Bigger Victim Than Myself

Bud Welch

∞

My only daughter was working in the Murrah Building in downtown Oklahoma City on April 19, 1995. When the bomb went off, it shook my house violently—eight miles from downtown. I couldn't imagine what had taken place.

A couple of minutes later, one of my younger brothers called to see if my television was on. I said no and he said, "Turn it on. Something has happened downtown." He was driving around the expressway and he could see a large plume of smoke rising. He turned his radio to a news station, and a couple of minutes later they said that there had been an explosion at the Federal Courthouse.

Within minutes, I had the television on and the traffic helicopters were still in the air from the morning rush hour; one of them was focusing on the Murrah Building from the north. I could see the whole face of the Murrah Building completely gone. My daughter, Julie, worked as a Spanish interpreter in that building on the first floor; when I saw that three-story pile of rubble, I frankly gave up any hope at that moment that Julie could have survived.

At nine o'clock in the morning Julie had left her work area in the rear of the building and walked forward to get her client who had been brought in by a friend. They had walked about halfway back to Julie's office when the bomb went off at 9:02. All three bodies were found together.

After Julie was killed, the absolute rage and revenge that went through me was gripping. I look back on the first four to five weeks after the bombing and call it a period of temporary insanity. I had started drinking and drank heavier and heavier. I was a smoker then; I reached the point of smoking three packs a day. By the end of January of 1996 I was literally hungover, if you will, twenty-four hours a day.

I went to the bomb site every single day after Julie had been killed, and on this particular day at the end of January, I was mentally and physically sick. I was stuck on April the nineteenth, 1995, and I needed to move forward in some way. I was unable to do that. So I began asking myself the question, what's it going to take? Do we need the trials to begin? (Neither trial started for more than two years after the bombing.) Do we need convictions? Do we need executions? Struggling with those question for two or three weeks after feeling the rage and revenge that I had, I finally realized that Julie and 167 others were dead in that great city because of the rage and revenge of convicted bomber Timothy McVeigh and coconspirator Terry Nichol. After being able to start sorting that out and start reconciling things, I was able to get my health back in shape.

Then one night, an image in the media of Timothy McVeigh's father, Bill, caught my attention. I remembered seeing Bill McVeigh on television during those first few weeks, that insanity period. There was a reporter in front of his home and Bill was standing by a flower bed. He's quite a large man, and he was stooped over as if he was maybe pulling weeds from the flower bed. I recall that at one point Bill stood almost straight up and looked into the lens of the television camera. When he did, I could see a man physically stooped in grief. I could see a deep pain in his eyes. I think most other people didn't recognize that pain, but I did because I was living that pain. I knew that someday for my own sanity I needed to go tell him that I truly cared how he felt and that I did not blame him or his family for what his son had done.

It took about four years, but a nun involved in prison ministry (near the McVeigh home in western New York state) eventually arranged such a meeting. I tried to learn what I could about Tim's father. I found out that he was a very shy person, didn't talk much. In the summertime, his hobby was growing a large garden. So when I knocked on his door, the first question I asked him was "Bill, I understand that you have a large garden in your backyard." If you'd have put a spotlight on that man's face, you could not have lit him up any more. And he did not seem the least bit shy to me at that moment. He simply said to me, "Yeah, would you like to see it?" I knew that he and I would find common ground, these two old men out there in the garden kicking dirt clods around. And we did.

Then we went inside and I met Tim's sister, Jennifer. I had seen Jennifer in the courtroom several times but had never met her. Jennifer sat at one end of the kitchen table and I sat at the other end. Bill sat to my left and there was this wall right next to the table that had some family photos on it, mainly just snapshots. The largest picture on that wall was an 8- by 10-inch portrait of Tim. During the hour-and-a-half that we visited, I periodically glanced at the wall—too many times. I started to feel self-conscious about it—wanting to know what *they* thought that *I* was thinking. So finally when I caught myself the next time, I just simply looked at the picture and I said, "What a good-looking kid." Well, there was silence in that kitchen when I said that.

After the silence ended, Bill looked at the wall and he simply said, "That's Tim's high school graduation picture." But when he did, a big old tear rolled out of his right eye.

I got ready to leave and shook Bill's hand. I extended my hand to Jennifer, and she didn't take my hand. She hugged me. We started crying and I began sobbing. It was like an uncontrolled sob. You don't know where you're going next or how to get out of the sob. So I just took her face in my hands and I simply said to her, "Honey, the three of us are in this for the rest of our lives. And we can make the most of it if we choose. I don't want your brother to die and I'll do everything that I can to prevent it."

We embraced again and after I left, I sobbed for probably forty-five minutes. But after I went through that process—and I call it a process because it was not a single event—it was as if this huge weight had been removed from my shoulders. And I've never felt closer to God than I did at that moment. What I found in western New York that Saturday morning was a bigger victim of the Oklahoma City bombing than myself.

∞

Bud Welch owned a small auto repair garage in Oklahoma City when his twenty-three-year-old daughter, Julie, was killed when bombs went off at the Murrah Federal Building. In the months after her death, Bud changed from supporting the death penalty for Timothy McVeigh and Terry Nichols, to taking a public stand against it. In 2001 Timothy McVeigh was executed for his part in the bombing. Welch is retired but continues to share the story of his daughter's life and death. He has participated in advocacy through Journey of Hope: From Violence to Healing *and other projects, and was interviewed by Jerry L. Holsopple for Mennonite Media's* Journey Toward Forgiveness *documentary, which aired on ABC-TV in 2001, from which this story was excerpted.*

Reconciliation

27

Chicken Soup

Ann Witman

∽

Scratch, scratch. Peck, peck. Those chickens were at it again, scouring the southern edge of our yard for seeds. The frozen February ground brought them out of the woods, across property lines in search of their next meal. Although the birds acted wild, they belonged to our neighbor.

At the time, the chickens were doing no harm. But as soon as the ground thawed my husband would fire up the red Case International and till our garden plot, located precisely over the spot where the chickens foraged. And when we planted our first green peas, we didn't intend for them to become chicken feed.

The offenders' owner lived in a double-wide trailer with a lean-to addition, dented corrugated metal and sagging decks, easily within view of my kitchen window through the bare trees. As my eyes moved back and forth from the chickens to the trailer, my thoughts turned to dogs, rifles, and fences.

Billy just wasn't the kind of neighbor who could be called approachable. In our six months of living there, we had barely exchanged more than a wave. No Trespassing signs lined his driveway, his expletives echoed throughout the neighborhood, and rumor had it that he regularly got drunk and beat his wife. So approaching Billy to discuss the behavior of his chickens did not seem realistic. The last thing I wanted to do was offend him.

Being allergic to dogs, my husband had long ago overruled any notions of having an indoor pet. But with two-and-a-half acres to patrol, an outside dog would have ample room to run, enjoy life, and not aggravate any allergies. And there would be plenty of recreation chasing chickens back to where they belonged. Was a dog our solution to the chicken invasion, disguised as a new pet for a young couple?

Hidden in a nook in our mud room stood a rifle. As long as the shooter took careful aim, a well-timed shot when Billy was gone for the evening would solve our chicken problem. A resulting dead chicken would be a liability, of course. Or perhaps a few missed shots would be enough to scare them off for the foreseeable future.

But a fence—now that would definitely take care of things. A decorative touch to our border, but most importantly, a permanent solution. The chickens would get the message without us ever having to speak to Billy. Good fences make good neighbors, right?

Sighing, I turned on the spigot and let cool water wash over the strawberries in my cupped hands. As much as I wanted to go compare the price of vinyl or wood at our home improvement store, something deep down didn't feel right. What had Billy done to me that I should withhold the dignity of a face-to-face encounter, the grace of a smile and conversation?

I looked up from the strawberries to his trailer, dim and foreboding in the barren winter scene. As the gentle stream ran through my fingers, I breathed a prayer for wisdom. The short walk from my house to his seemed longer than ever before. But when I glanced down again, I suddenly sensed what I should do. I finished washing a handful of berries and put them back into the green plastic pint container.

My fingers stiffly zipped my winter coat. I grasped my peace offering and prayed all the way across the hard ground, hoping I wasn't putting us in harm's way. The chickens scattered in front of me, a flurry of feathers and scrawny legs. I tried to rehearse my lines as my feet carried me ahead of my rational thoughts.

I stepped carefully onto the uneven front deck, avoiding the rotting splintered boards. I surveyed the door, its peeling gray paint matching the feel of the dead winter air and the tone of my spirit. Was I foolish to approach the person inside? He wouldn't dare hurt me, would he?

I knocked faintly and looked down. An empty beer bottle lay at my feet. The washed berries suddenly felt icy in my hands. The door knob slowly turned, and the creak of rusty hinges and wafting stale smoke jostled my senses awake.

"Oh, hi, Billy, you may not know me, but my husband and I built the house next door. I'm Sarah."

Steel blue eyes pierced through wrinkles that clung to the edges of his weathered face.

"I brought you some strawberries." I willed my cold cheeks to rise in a smile and extended the gift in my trembling hands.

Billy's worn fingers closed around the container. "Thank ya." His lips parted to reveal an incomplete row of tobacco-stained teeth that dotted his smile. "Say, I been meanin' to get my chickens outta yer yard. I caught some, but those darn things are all up roostin' in the woods and they're wild as can be. I'll make sure they ain't botherin' ya no more come spring."

My rehearsed lines hadn't prepared me for this. "Oh, wow, thank you." Suddenly Billy didn't seem so scary. "We like chickens, but we do want to plant a garden and would hate for them to dig up the seeds."

"Don't ya'll worry none, I'll have 'em out soon. Just gotta catch 'em all. An' if ya need to, just shoot 'em." He chuckled softly.

"Well, we appreciate you trying to catch them. And I hope you enjoy the strawberries."

My feet glided home. The air didn't seem so bitterly cold anymore. Over the next few days, I watched the number of chickens dwindle to just three, particularly skittish and independent. Cleaning the last of the strawberries one afternoon, I heard the doorbell ring. To my surprise, I wasn't afraid when I saw Billy standing there.

He thrust a plastic grocery bag toward me and grinned shyly. "Ya'll like chicken?"

"Sure," I said as I slowly opened the bag. A rubbery lump of white bumpy skin was spattered with pale splashes of blood.

"It's one I caught. I cleaned it fer ya."

I found my breath as I realized the gift he was offering me. "Thank you, Billy. That is very kind."

"I'll git the rest of 'em soon, so y'all can plant yer garden."

"Thank you. We'll be sure to share our vegetables with you this summer. And we really appreciate the chicken."

My pressure cooker softened that tough, scrawny chicken, once running around in our yard, until it melted in our mouths. I've never tasted better chicken soup, seasoned with grace that my wary heart had never expected to receive.

∞

Ann Witman is a pseudonym for an East Coast writer, currently in seminary and married with two children.

28

Right Where God Wants Us to Be

David Chow

⌇

I didn't always get along with my dad. My mom would say that we are very much alike and that's why we butted heads. I think it all began when he first asked me, "So, what do you want to be when you grow up?"

I loved my grandpa. I adored him. He was my hero. I wanted to be just like him. "I want to be a missionary . . . " I could see the angst scratch across my dad's face as he strongly suggested, "No. No. You want to be a doctor, a businessman, or even a lawyer, eh? Your grandpa was a lawyer. He was trained as a lawyer in Cambridge, England."

But God called him to be a missionary. In China. Yes, he was of Chinese extraction, but he didn't even speak a word of Chinese! The remarkable thing was that my grandpa, like his ten siblings, born and raised in British Guyana, didn't speak a word of Cantonese, but he spoke the Queen's English.

I'm sure they enjoyed life before Grandpa took his little family across the globe into unknown lands during very uncertain times. Grandpa was a lawyer. Grandma was a dentist. They enjoyed a standard of living few of their generation and ethnic extraction experienced until they were called to be missionaries in Shanghai.

My dad was born in 1939 in Shanghai, China, about the time the Japanese military invaded. Dad spoke more Chinese than my grandpa ever did! Life was hard in China. Not much to eat, and lots of Japanese soldiers, certainly persecution. My dad grew up hating the Japanese soldiers. He remembers beheadings and stories of the "comfort" women who serviced the servicemen. The experience hardened his heart. Due to their British passports, when it got really bad, they were able to flee back to the Commonwealth in South America.

Ever since I was about eight years old, I had a deep sense that I was being called to serve on the mission field or in pastoral ministry. It was a conviction. My youth pastor worked out a scholarship for me to attend Bible college in Saskatchewan. Many of my friends left to study there. But Dad said, "I want you to go to *real* school. Get a *real* education."

Every fiber of my being wanted to go to the Bible college. But, as an obedient firstborn son, I obeyed. I entered university but, to my father's disappointment, graduated with a French degree. Later I married my university sweetheart. Charlene was just graduating from her studies, when I asked if she'd be open to traveling—serving on a short-term mission with Mennonite Brethren Missions and Services International in Japan. They needed English as a Second Language teachers. "Sure, go ahead and apply," she said.

Only a couple of weeks later, we got the call. Charlene answered the phone and began shaking. We talked and prayed. I told her that we wouldn't go unless she felt the call to go herself. After a couple weeks of deep prayer, she said,

"I'm ready to go." We consulted with our home-group, our church, and our families. My dad was livid.

The day before our commissioning service, he took me out for breakfast. I thought he was going to wish me well, pray for me. Instead, he said, "You're making a big mistake. You're a bad son, and a bad husband." His words broke my heart.

On the day of the commissioning, my dad wouldn't even look me in the eye. I just saw bloodshot eyes. Anger? Sadness? Perhaps even fear? I don't even remember my parents being at the airport the day we left. I do remember my father-in-law's crushing hug as tears went down his cheeks.

Japan was an incredible place to minister. Lots of new things to experience and a beautifully loyal people. However, they did ask me, "Why are you here?" "Don't you know what our people did to your people?" "How does your family feel about you coming here?"

Why does it take thousands of miles away from home, someone else, through a translator, to make my father's feelings suddenly dawn on me? I'd entered the lion's den. My dad didn't want me coming back to such a difficult place. He must have been so angry and so . . . hurt. He'd lost his son to . . . *them.*

After about a year, I declared that I couldn't possibly head into ministry without reconciling with my dad. I decided to write him a letter, telling him that I was sorry about the things I said, and the things I didn't say. I needed to apologize. I just wanted to begin again.

I got a letter back. This, from a person who had previously written to me once, perhaps twice, in my entire life. It said, "Dear David, I want to thank you for your apology. I forgive you. Will you forgive me?" I was in shock. "By the way, I know you want to pursue seminary studies. Let me know which schools you're interested in and I'll look them up for you. . . ." My jaw dropped. "And I don't want to fight with God anymore. I want you to be happy and I bless you in your decision to pursue full-time ministry." I couldn't stop the tears from coming. I could have died a happy man right then. That day, I came to understand what it means to receive *the blessing*. I still have that letter in my journal.

As our two-year term was drawing to a close, about forty to fifty Japanese brothers and sisters in Christ wanted to come back with us to Canada so that they could see our homeland, our churches, and meet our families. But my father still would have nothing to do with them. "No one is going to be staying at our house," he said.

My in-laws have a large acreage, so they hosted a number of our visitors. Our home church in Calgary billeted many more. Charlene's parents also hosted a big barbecue supper for all the visitors. My parents were invited. We thought that this would be a nonthreatening place for them to interact with our Japanese friends. You have to understand that while in Japan there were about ten women who took us under their wings, took it upon themselves to be our Japanese "moms." Short and petite, but very dignified, they came and bowed before my dad—nose to the ground—and through a translator said, "Mr. Chow, we thank you for sending us your son and daughter-in-law to serve us. We are very blessed. We humbly thank you very much."

My dad's jaw dropped. And the walls around his heart began to crack. At that moment, I understood that God used us not only as ministers of grace in Japan, but as his instruments in a much larger opus than I could ever have imagined.

My dad used to have a large book that sat on the coffee table in the living room, *The Rape of Nanking*. Not the most compelling conversational piece one could have in the home. After that barbecue, the book was put away in the back closet. He began driving Japanese vehicles!

God was at work when I was a young child. He was working when I struggled to find my calling. He was working when my dad was struggling with his own thoughts of the past, and God was working as we served in Japan—

ultimately bringing our friends to meet our families. Grace upon grace upon grace.

∞

David Chow and his wife, Charlene, live in cosmopolitan Vancouver, British Columbia. Dave serves as pastor of Killarney Park Mennonite Brethren Church, an intentionally intercultural fellowship. He loves sushi, and he loves his dad.

29

Testing My Peace Stance

Bruce Stambaugh

∞

The first sermon I heard in a Mennonite church was on nonresistance. That was exactly what I was looking for spiritually, and I embraced it. My father, a World War II veteran, was skeptical but eventually accepted my decision.

Now, four decades later, I was to accompany my eighty-nine-year-old father on a special excursion called Honor Flight for World War II vets. Dad was dying of cancer, and he had long wanted to make this trip to Washington, D.C. Regardless of physical condition, each of the 117 vets on the plane was required to have a guardian for the all-day round trip. In his situation, Dad needed extra care.

Given my stance on war, I was reluctant to go. I likely would be the only conscientious objector on the packed plane. But this trip wasn't about me. It was about my father's fulfilling one of his dreams. To help him accomplish that, regardless of my personal convictions, I needed to go with him.

As anticipated, the vets received their patriotic due. Upon arriving at Reagan National Airport in Washington, D.C., fire trucks sprayed arches of water across our arriving jet-liner. This ritual was usually reserved for dignitaries. As we entered the terminal, a concert band played patriotic music. Red, white, and blue balloons were everywhere, and hundreds of vigorous volunteers greeted us.

At the circular marble World War II memorial just completed in 2004, strangers shook hands with the vets and thanked them for their service. I took it all in, focusing my attention on caring for my elderly father.

After visiting other war monuments in the capital, we flew home to the airport we had left just hours earlier. There the vets received a similar patriotic welcome home. Dad said this experience ranked right behind his sixty-seven-year marriage.

Especially after that comment, I was elated that I had had the chance to experience that day with my father. I felt honored to have been able to accompany him on his most significant day, and I was glad he had gotten to go. Dad died three months later.

Despite all the hoopla of the day or perhaps because of it, the futility of war became all the more obvious to me. All the vets said they hated what they had had to do in the war. I also remembered the words of Jesus, who said to turn the other cheek and to go the second mile and beyond for your enemy.

The trip with my father was an inspirational reminder of the commitment I had made as a young man to a different way of making peace in a hostile world. Even though my convictions would not have let me serve in the war, I nevertheless bonded with my father in his time of need, and I greatly respected his courage and devotion to his country.

I had participated in the Honor Flight out of love and respect for my earthly father. I had held fast to my peace convictions out of love and devotion to my Father in heaven. In that paradox, I had found no conflict whatsoever, only grace and a different kind of peace.

∞

Bruce Stambaugh is a retired educator, newspaper colum-nist, and freelance writer. He lives near Millersburg, Ohio, where he attends Millersburg Mennonite Church.

Trust

30

Lost Boy

Gareth Brandt

∞

There I was, a veteran youth pastor sitting at a youth workers' retreat, listening to the speaker talk about how to understand and counsel youth who had been victims of sexual abuse. Then something began to awaken inside me. I awoke to the nightmarish reality that I was the abused kid he was talking about.

That retreat is now more than two decades in the past, but it was the beginning of a long and difficult journey of healing from childhood sexual abuse that has become a significant part of my personal spiritual formation and my ministry to youth and young adults.

When I was a boy, there was a young man in our community who taught me all I ever knew about sports and how to play them. Unfortunately, this relationship was blemished by sleepovers at his house, where I was raped and sexually abused. Because I idolized him, I did not question him on anything. There was no language of sexual abuse in my world at the time it happened to me. There was no way for me to cry out to someone for help or to say, "This hurts, this is wrong, don't do this to me." Therefore, the pain went down deep inside for many years and got lost in the cobwebs of my memory until adulthood.

Kids who are abused sexually or otherwise have lost their childhood innocence. They have been robbed of it and are left with a bag of scars and memories they are unable to deal with. There are numerous self-protective defense mechanisms that victims use in order to survive the trauma of abuse. An abused child is not able to fully experience the emotions of pain, fear, or rage that are associated with abuse. If they were to do so, they would go crazy. As a consequence, the terrible memories and accompanying emotions are often blocked or repressed involuntarily until adulthood. Denial or rationalization of the experiences will often accompany this repression: "It happened so long ago," "Worse things have happened to others," "Maybe it was all just a bad dream," "He really didn't mean anything by it." These were phrases that I used for years.

Survivors of childhood abuse sometimes become excellent people-helpers themselves. In a strange sort of way, helping other people to deal with their pain becomes a way to avoid facing one's own. That was who I was: I became a caring and outgoing youth pastor. However, at that retreat I began to realize that I was, in fact, the abused kid with low self-esteem who needed the ministry of healing.

A few years after the retreat, I went to a spiritual director to get help for the spiritual stream that had run dry within me. I was expecting some accountability for my spiritual disciplines or some advice on how to pray better. Instead, I was led to the mirror of my soul to look at myself and the wounds of my past.

My spiritual director was a retired woman who had gone through her own pain as a child, a wife, and as a single mother. Now, she was in a place of deep strength and could offer grace and healing to me. The Spirit was the surgeon and she became the midwife to the new man who was being born. Her calm words and strong hands steadied me in my faltering journey toward healing. She was literally there for me as a counselor and guide.

Through this counseling, the emotions that I was unable to experience as a child and as a teenager came roaring to life. It started with terrifying nightmares and irrational fears and moved to feelings of deep pain, loss, and betrayal. I was a powerful and successful man in the exterior world: I had a successful youth pastorate with a growing ministry and good relations with colleagues and congregation; a loving and supportive wife; three healthy children; a house; and a minivan. What more could a man want? But pain does not discriminate. On the inside, I became a little lost boy, feeling for the first time the full terror and hurt of my childhood wounds.

Death and numbness seemed almost pleasant realities in the midst of this terror and pain. I felt the loss of my childhood innocence and the betrayal of my boyhood hero. If life were to be described in climatic seasons, autumn and winter became the perpetual seasons of my spirituality. Sometimes I would have liked to "fly south" to escape the difficult aspects of my healing.

The road to healing is often different than one might expect. For victims of abuse, it often comes through anger and empowerment. I found it very difficult to be angry with my abuser, but for real healing to happen I had to leave the role of the victim. Jesus is angry when the human temple of the Spirit is desecrated, and he called me to place the responsibility where it belonged: with the abuser. The silence and the darkness of the evil tomb of abuse had to be broken!

My spiritual director had me imagine Jesus catching my abuser in the act of raping me, saying, "What was Jesus' reaction at the desecration of the temple? Your body is the temple of the Holy Spirit!" I imagined Jesus grabbing him by the genitals and throwing him out of the bedroom window. Through this and other rituals I was beginning to get in touch with my emotions in a constructive and healing way.

I ended up regaining my childhood innocence; the lost boy was found. I felt like a calf released from the stall in spring after waiting a long, dark winter. I reclaimed my given name, Gareth, which I had shortened and changed in my teenage years, affirmed by the young man who was both my hero and my abuser. I still hear the voice of my spiritual director calling me "Gareth" for the first time since I was a child. I was born again—a grown man, free and empowered to be who I was created and named to be. Mysteriously, God used the most terrible thing in my life to bring new insight, joy, and meaning to my life and ministry.

∞

Gareth Brandt is the author of Under Construction: Reframing Men's Spirituality *(Herald Press, 2010) and professor of practical theology at Columbia Bible College in Abbotsford, British Columbia, where he lives with his wife, Cynthia. They have one daughter, three sons, and one daughter-in-law. He enjoys cycling, gardening, folk music, and reading poetry out loud.*

31

Birds in the Night

Edna Krueger Dyck

൦

I really didn't want to go to Jerusalem. I was scared. Yes, I was intrigued with the idea of living where Jesus had lived, seeing the sites mentioned in the stories I had heard and read since I was a child. Nazareth, Cana, the garden of Gethsemane—there was a mystery in those names I wished I could experience. "To walk where Jesus walked" sounded so exciting and wonderful. But . . . the Middle East was such a political powder keg, where things could explode at any minute, and I really didn't want to be there when it did.

It was 1990 and Mennonite Central Committee (MCC) had invited my husband and me to spend several months living and working in Jerusalem on a special assignment. As we prepared to leave, suddenly the headlines screamed, "Saddam Hussein Invades Kuwait." There were threats and counterthreats being hurled; the first Gulf War was imminent. What now? Surely they wouldn't ask us to leave the relative safety of the United States when war was imminent! We called the MCC representative in Jerusalem and he said, "Oh sure, come on down, things are always like this here. We are very excited to have you come and stay with us." It was not what I wanted to hear.

We went in spite of Saddam Hussein. And it was truly amazing to be in the "holy land." I read the Gospel stories with new interest, visualizing how and where the incidents described might have happened. A new love and awe for Christ crept over me as I walked the ancient streets, stopping at the stations of the cross on the Via Dolorosa, touching the rock where tradition held that his body had been laid. We visited several "Easter" sites where it is possible that Mary encountered the angel and heard the words: "Why do you seek the living among the dead?" Jesus' life, death, and resurrection took on a whole new significance. It was an experience I shall never forget.

My initial apprehension and fear did not recede, however. Our Palestinian friends whom we encountered in the neighborhood where we lived told stories of the oppression and hardship they lived with. They regularly implored us as Americans to tell the world about these difficulties. We lived a short ten-minute walk up the hill from the Damascus Gate leading into the old city. Each day brought exciting adventures and new insights into my holy history, but I was partially paralyzed by fear. In our explorations into that fascinating city we encountered fully armed Israeli soldiers patrolling the streets. We witnessed Palestinian children being tear-gassed on their way home from school. We occasionally saw settlers, confidently shouldering automatic rifles, roaming the streets. Palestinians and Israelis alike looked on us foreigners with suspicion. We heard about skirmishes in the streets; words like *intifada*, *bombings*, *murders* were part of our everyday conversation. Then there was the "October massacre" when twelve Palestinians were killed on Temple Mount, the site of the mosque that was so important to the Palestinian people. I often thought and sometimes said, "Let's go back to Kansas."

Then one night I was awakened by a curious sound. The sound was unmistakable; there were birds chirping, singing, carrying on rather loudly, under our bedroom window in the middle of the night. I couldn't tell whether they were sparrows, but the Matthew verse about two sparrows being sold for a penny and a human life being worth more than many sparrows came to mind (Matthew 10:28-31). I remembered that Jesus had been telling the disciples about their precarious future as his emissaries and had been trying to allay their fears. They can kill your bodies, but they cannot kill your souls, he had said.

I can't really say that I was not afraid in Jerusalem again, but my state of mind changed that night. I knew that my life was worth more than "many sparrows." On hearing those cheerful creatures under the window, a feeling of deep peace came over me. And I knew that death for me, should it take place in Jerusalem, was not to be feared.

I learned two things that night. First, birds sometimes sing at night. Second, I don't mind being wakened when God has a message for me.

∞

Edna Krueger Dyck, trained as a teacher and educator, worked as an editor and copy editor in the former General Conference Mennonite Church office. She is also a retired pastor. A Canadian by birth, she and her husband have lived in Kansas since 1965. Edna is the mother of four adult children and grandmother of four grandsons and one granddaughter. She is a member of Shalom Mennonite Church in Newton, Kansas.

32

Grace: God's Care and Provision

Sandi Marr

❧

During World War II my grandparents, Howard and Elva Fretz, were very interested in supporting world relief programs. Through Grandpa's exporting of cattle to southern Pennsylvania, he learned of Brethren Service headquartered in New Windsor, Maryland. Brethren Service was shipping bred two-year-old heifers to Germany. Grandpa was enthralled with this project. It was dubbed "Heifer Project" because of its perpetuity (now Heifer International). A heifer was given to a German family who had lost all of its animals in the war with the understanding that its first heifer calf born would be given to a neighbor who suffered the same loss.

Grandpa, who was accustomed to buying cattle in southern Ontario and exporting them, promoted this project by getting Brethren in Christ congregations to pay for a heifer, which he would purchase and then arrange shipment to

Pennsylvania. Brethren Service organized the collection of the cattle and secured young men to serve as "cowboys," the deckhands to care for the cattle. The shipping costs of the livestock and ocean travel costs of the young men were covered by an agency of the United Nations. One day, Grandpa approached his son, my dad.

"Lester," he said, "have you ever thought about applying with Brethren Service to accompany a shipload of heifers to Europe?"

Dad was nineteen years old and in the midst of completing grade thirteen. He decided to submit an application along with a required essay on pacifism. Dad's application was among hundreds of others received. Some of his friends and classmates discouraged him, saying, "You are crazy, Lester! Leaving grade thirteen will put you a year behind everyone else."

But Dad was excited to be accepted. He began his preparations to leave.

Grandpa sold a cow and gave Dad the three hundred dollars he received. Dad bought a used navy blue suit, a 35 mm camera, and a quantity of film and flashbulbs. His family gave him a suitcase as an early Christmas present. He left home with $220 his wallet. The navy suit was required to sail with officer's status since Dad did not belong to the seamen's union. The officers wore dress uniform for each meal. Dad was obliged to do the same.

Knowing that he had free return travel back to New York, before leaving home, Dad carefully tucked seventeen dollars in the back of his wallet to cover his return train fare to Buffalo, New York, where family would meet him.

The next three months of the assignment would prove to be life changing. Dad saw and experienced things he never dreamed or imagined. He lived and worked with many different people. While in Germany, Dad volunteered for Brethren Service and Mennonite Central Committee in food distribution and a building project. In addition to accompanying the shipment of heifers, Dad had amazing opportunities that included riding a ski lift to the top of an Austrian Alp, taking a gondola through the canals of Venice, and seeing Paris from the Eiffel Tower.

After spending nearly three months on this assignment, it was time for Dad to return home. The U.S. Lines *Harvester* on which dad sailed docked at Pier 60 on the East River in New York, and suddenly Dad realized he had no idea how he would get from Pier 60 to Grand Central Station. He was overwhelmed with fear and panic about the final leg of his journey. Because it was Lincoln's birthday, everything was very quiet. Dad's three suitcases sat lonely on the dock beside the gangplank.

After a difficult time being cleared by customs and immigration, a gruff custom's officer said, "Now retrieve your luggage and be on your way!"

Dad had no idea where he was going, but as he bent down to pick up his luggage, he heard his name called. When he looked up, to his amazement, a friendly man suddenly appeared out of nowhere.

"Lester!" the man said.

Dad immediately recognized the voice to be that of Thurl Metzger, the executive director of Brethren Service.

Dad breathed a huge sigh of relief; someone he knew was on this desolate dock. How comforting to see a familiar face. Cordial greetings were exchanged.

Then Mr. Metzger asked, "How are you getting home?"

Hesitantly Dad explained, "I plan to take a train to Buffalo. But I have no idea how to get to Grand Central Station from here."

Sensing Dad's dilemma, Mr. Metzger hailed a cab. He offered to ride with Dad to the train station and also graciously paid the fare.

As they rode together, Dad curiously inquired, "How did you know about my arrival plans?"

Mr. Metzger replied, "We have ways of knowing."

Dad tried repeatedly to ascertain how Mr. Metzger was aware of his arrival.

Mr. Metzger simply repeated, "We have ways of knowing."

Dad could only deduce that God sent Mr. Metzger to be a gracious blessing to the end of a very significant chapter of his teenage life. We can trust God to lead us in all circumstances of life.

∽

Sandi Marr lives in Welland, Ontario, with her husband, Robert. They have four young adult children and eight grandchildren. Sandi and Robert attend Wainfleet Brethren in Christ Church where they share their gifts on the worship team. Over the past thirty years, Sandi has found enrichment through writing and congregational ministry. Sandi studied in Israel and Palestine and received a master's degree in theological studies from Conrad Grebel University College, Waterloo, Ontario. Sandi was born in Zimbabwe where her parents, Mary and Lester Fretz, served with Brethren in Christ missions. Sandi enjoys living close to her parents who are now in their eighties.

33

When We Ask, "Why?"

Alvin Ens

⬭

One Saturday evening we received the first of several telephone calls. I answered but heard only banging and noise in the background such as a household might have. We received two more such anonymous calls within the space of an hour. No matter how often we said "hello," there was no answer on the other end of the line.

Early Sunday morning, at six o'clock, our bedside telephone rang four times on my wife's nightstand before I stretched from my side of the bed to answer the nuisance call. There was no communication, but I could hear a child banging in the background. It rang two or three more times in the next fifteen minutes.

I was wide awake, yet my wife had not answered the phone. It was then that I realized that she, a diabetic, was having a hypoglycemic reaction. I brought her some honey to swallow to stabilize her blood sugar. She was soon fine.

We don't have a caller ID display on our telephone; however, it seemed to be the same caller each time. Later in the day, our son suggested using Star 69 (where you just dial those digits, *-6-9, which incurs a small charge) to trace the call. Sunday evening, when the nuisance call came again, my wife traced it with the Star 69 procedure. It was the household of an associate of mine who had programmed my number into his cell phone, and his child had been playing with it. They apologized; it was not a big deal.

Was it just an annoyance, an accidental call made by a child? Was it a coincidence that my wife needed sugar at the time the telephone rang at six o'clock in the morning?

Normally at night, I can sense my wife's restlessness if she is low on sugar. Not so on that Sunday morning. Yet I got the message. How? By a child playing with a cell phone. I believe it was God's intervention.

The conventional wisdom of this world is confounded by God. The apostle Paul said to the Corinthians that "the wisdom of this world is foolishness in God's sight" (1 Corinthians 3:19 NIV).

I don't know how God uses the coincidences in this life for his purposes. But I believe that God used a little child playing with a cell phone to alert me that my wife needed help in the early hours of a Sunday morning. Some might ask why God would alert us and save my wife's life, yet not protect someone else from a terrible accident. There are no easy answers, which I pondered through another incident.

One summer I was in Vancouver General Hospital in the intensive care unit being observed for a brain hemorrhage. My nurse told me the room next door would be occupied by a lady who was "very sick."

The woman arrived in a flurry of activity. Later that night, underneath the curtain, I saw her bed wheeled out. A scrub-down and thorough mop-up of the room ensued.

I asked my nurse in the morning, "The lady in the next room didn't make it, did she?"

Her reply was straightforward, "No, she didn't."

I was left among the living, and I asked myself why not her, why me? I had probably seen more days; I was less worthy of a continued life. God works in mysterious ways. I thanked God I was still alive.

I was unable to answer a simple question of "Why me, God?" Why was I given time to see my family again? I have several uncompleted projects. Was I given time to finish them? My church, my family, and my associates prayed for me. Was it the power of prayer? Was my time just not up? I do not know. I do know this: I have been given another opportunity at life.

Perhaps I live to tell my wife what a wonderful mate she has been to me, especially in times of medical adversity. Maybe I am alive and in the hospital to be the guru to a young physiotherapist who asks me one day, "What is the difference between a Methodist and a Mennonite?" or the next question, whether I believe in eternal security.

The "Why me?" question has been around as long as humankind. Sometimes we phrase it negatively as "Why me? Why did I have to have a stroke?" To phrase it more positively, "Why me? Why do I continue to live?"

I get one more turn at affirming life. God has given me another opportunity to live. The Creator of life has continued to give life to me to use in my latter days, in the next year. I do not know for how long. I simply know I have life for today. Praise God.

∽◌

Alvin G. Ens dabbles in prose and poetry. He writes, edits, and mentors. He freelances for both religious and secular media, both popular and scholarly. He is a retired high school English teacher. He has published eight books of poetry, family history, and fiction. He is a member of his local poetry group, Poets Potpourri Society, and Fraser Valley Christian Writers. He and Irene have just celebrated their fortieth wedding anniversary and have three children and two grandchildren. They attend Level Ground Mennonite Church in Abbotsford, British Columbia.

Calling

34

Home to the Red House

Jim Wallis

∞

I live in a poor neighborhood. I know people who have been waiting for low-income housing for years. Their kids get older every single year, living in very dangerous and difficult and insecure circumstances.

When my children were just three and seven years old, we had just come back from speaking at a Church of the Brethren youth conference. My three-year-old kept saying, "Are we going back to our red house?"

And I was able to say, "Yeah." He said "Great, we'll be home, back in our red house." To have a house that these two boys know is their house, their place to live, is very important to them—very important to any child. Home should be a place of special grace.

We travel all over the world, but they always talk about going back to the red house. It's part of their security, their stability, part of their knowing a sense of place, part of a community. They love to travel with us, but they love to come home.

What does it mean not to have a red house, or any color house, and not even to know where you're going be living? I know families living in shelters. I can't imagine what that means for school, for bedtime, for reading stories at night, for all the things that we assume as parents. Kids need stability; if there is no safe place to live, they lack a basic stability.

A woman named Thelma lived next door to me. She had lived there for years before we moved there. Her husband had died. We figured out one day that she had paid for that house four times over in rent. But she could never afford to buy it, never afford the down payment. She was paying the "mortgage payment" as a rental payment. But she didn't have a middle-class family that says, "Let me get you started in the housing market." She didn't have what middle-class moms and dads do for their kids.

I had been gone for six weeks in extended speaking and came home one day to learn that Thelma was gone. The Washington, D.C., government now owned her house. They had raised her rent and they wouldn't fix the plumbing or the leaky roof, and she had to leave. So she lost any equity in that home for her kids' education (as well as missing the middle-class home owner's tax deduction). She lost all that. That place became a crack house that we had to fight for years—rats and drugs were in there. It's not rocket science to figure out how Thelma could have owned her own home. We could have made financing for a down payment possible for Thelma.

I'll tell the story of another woman and all her kids who were going to be evicted illegally. We stood with her in court and got it overturned, so she got to stay until the rats invaded the house. I mean big rats. I went in with cowboy boots and a baseball bat, going after rats. And then one day, one of the rats got into the crib of baby Isaac. One of the other kids scooped Isaac out before he was bitten by the rat. So they moved in with us and stayed for a year. Ten kids, mom and dad, and six of us, one bathroom. It was quite a year. I learned a lot about housing issues for poor families during that year. Then we became involved in a housing ministry that basically was creating tenant units inside apartments, that got tenants the first right of refusal if an opportunity came to buy. We turned about ten of those apartments into tenant-owned cooperatives out of that experience. So we've been able to see and feel these issues as we get to know people.

It is really important for kids to have safe, secure places to live. Any parent knows that. Let's make sure we care about all kids, not just our own, having a safe and decent place to live.

As an evangelical Christian, I insist that fighting poverty is a moral values issue too. The Bible talks more about our obligations to poor people than any other social issue. So this should be at the very top of our list of what Christians ought to care about. If we care about families and kids, we must care about them living in safe, secure places so they can grow and be all that God wants them to be.

The left and the right argue about poverty. They debate who's responsible, blaming each other for poverty. When the blaming's done, the talking stops, and people continue to be poor. There are 9.2 million American families (2006 figures) with somebody in the household who is a full-time worker, and yet they are still poor. They are working hard and falling short. That includes 20 million children. This is just simply wrong to me. From a biblical point of view, it's wrong. So how do we change things so that every kid can come home to a safe and secure place?

∞

Jim Wallis is a Christian writer and political activist. He is best known as the founder and editor of Sojourners *magazine and the founder of the Washington, D.C.,-based Christian community of the same name. Wallis is well known for his advocacy on issues of peace and social justice. He is the father of two children and married to the Reverend Joy Carroll. Excerpted from an interview with Jim Wallis by Sheri Hartzler for a documentary produced by Mennonite Media,* Building on Faith: Making Poverty Housing History.

35

Fired

Marty Troyer

∞

Few things have formed me as pastor like being told I should not be one.

I had embraced a pastoral identity since called as a teenager, had sacrificed myself and my family countless times to perform, and had tirelessly worked to hold it all together. And in one unexpected meeting that was ripped from my soul, seemingly doing irreparable damage.

"We think it's time for you to resign" reverberated loudly off the walls of my heart as "Fired!" "Not good enough!" "Worthless!" "Weakest Link!" "Failure!" All labels that created in me a new default mode of deep shame and anger, a sense of nothingness that comes when your vocation is taken from you unwillingly. The "nothingness" shamed me so greatly it was two days before I could share the story with my wife or close friends. I felt it so pervasively I expressed it in the clothes I chose to wear and by growing a beard to mask my inward broken reality.

I initially directed my angst at two sources: *God* and *church*.

My theology and spirituality underwent an almost instantaneous transformation. Images of God as "Savior" in one's moment of need, or the answer to prayers, ceased making sense. God, it was now clear, could no longer be trusted because God was not personal. I internalized and "tried on" the psalmist's cries as if they were true: "Has [God's] steadfast love ceased forever? Are [God's] promises at an end for all time? Has God forgotten to be gracious?" (Psalms 77:8-9). At the time in my life when I needed faith more than ever, I felt abandoned and alone.

I also felt deserted by a church system that valued productivity over people. Being identified as the weakest link, marked for necessary sacrifice, conjured my own childhood abuse, leaving me feeling similarly exposed and expendable. The pain of rejection was greatly intensified as the wounds were inflicted by trusted Christian leaders.

Isn't it supposed to be different in the church? Perhaps. But my experience suggested the church had a low interest in good pastors being healthy people. And so as easily as I was blamed, I fired back, placing the blame outside myself.

This was ironic, because it was only days before I heard the word *resign* that I had bargained with God that I myself was ready to resign unless something drastic changed soon in a job I never really enjoyed. And, in all fairness, I was not very good at it either. I felt like the caricature on stage, frantically spinning dozens of plates while pathetically knowing deep down this was not what I was made to do.

Was this what it meant to be a pastor? Was this what organizational ministry demanded? Is this what Jesus envisioned when he asked Peter to "feed my sheep"? If so, I found myself profoundly uninterested.

So how in the world did I ever risk congregational ministry again? It didn't happen overnight. In fact, six years later, I still live the story as I continue to explore the breadth of grace that comes with finding myself a pastor yet again.

Instead of destroying my sense of vocation, this event galvanized a level of internal transformation I could not have accomplished alone and for which I'm forever thankful.

Did my transformation happen in worship and a radical reorientation to God's actions in our world? This crisis revealed a shift that had already occurred inside me, a shift I had been unwilling to live into. Worship over the next years oriented me to the beautiful new world God was creating out of the midst of the old. It repeatedly invited me (even me!) to be part of its coming transformation. Indeed, though my theology underwent painful heart surgery, I had not, after all, "lost" my faith. It had merely grown and developed, drastically enlarging my heart and capacity for caring.

Did my transformation happen through radical new formation practices and deep vulnerability with self and community? The familiar practice of prayer held little grace; it was time for brutal honesty with self and God. *The Leader's Journey*, written by Jim Herrington, R. Robert Creech, and Trisha Taylor, says this well, "Do not look to external symptoms. Look at your own life. Look at your own responsibility. Look at how you have contributed to the circumstances around you, and hear my call to the radical repentance that results in your own personal transformation" (6, 8). This message was the terrible beauty that proved to be "like fire in my bones."

Did my transformation happen when I refused to be defined by outside expectations—salvation by social acceptance—and embraced by God alone: "By grace you have been saved"? I could finally say, "This is who I am, this is what I offer: nothing more, nothing less. It is enough." This story has freed me to guard the limits of my vocation of radically following Jesus deeper into community and mission. It also has provided strength to resist the temptations of ministry disconnected from discipleship. The transitions from youth to lead pastor, from large to small church, from the geographical center to the margins, and from rural to urban ministries were categorical changes creating space for hope.

Did it happen after a smooth first year that was filled with affirmation? Or was it five years to the day of being asked to resign, when new leadership gathered to share the results of an overwhelmingly positive review process? When I was offered a new five-year contract (rather than the traditional three), I felt the hole of "nothingness" close for good, and the tectonic plates of my soul shifted. A new, outward expression replaced the beard that was now long gone—with my head held high in an overwhelming sweep of grace and dignity, I'd forgotten it was missing.

I cannot tell you when God brought new hope and life into my being. But I can tell you I am being transformed by God's grace. The emotional maturity that grace creates has rippled through my entire congregation. Our congregational meetings, church worship (planning and practicing), and leadership team meetings have all gone through drastic change as I have traded the need to perform for pastoring in grace.

Grace is freeing me from the tyranny of expertise so that I can assume a listening posture, one that sees collective wisdom as more holistic than anything I have to offer alone, and where creativity flourishes. We see this perhaps most clearly in how a new table-based format in congregational meetings has empowered the voice of everyone present, drained our decision-making of anxiety, and engendered deeper commitment and ownership in the vision and direction of our congregation.

Only God knows if I could have become a healthy pastor without being asked to resign. But one thing I do know, in and through following Christ on this journey (including the dark valley of resignation), *I am a pastor*. This is my faith. This is my hope.

∽

Marty Troyer is the pastor of Houston Mennonite Church in Houston, Texas. He loves his totally normal (and therefore amazing!) family, encouraging people to become what they were created to be, and dreaming about what Houston could look like if we truly worked to make God's "kingdom come on earth as it is in heaven." Marty blogs as "The Peace Pastor" for The Houston Chronicle *at blog.chron .com/thepeacepastor/.*

36

A Heart That Lasts Forever

Joan Clayton

∞

I believed every child in my room was not there by accident, but placed by God. Each one became my forever
friend, a love I could never let go. Such was Robert.

He came to my second grade classroom with his older
married sister; he was the interpreter. He found his name-
tag and seated himself while placing his supplies just so
on his desk. Those big black eyes told me volumes and his
broad smile welcomed me into his young life.

Robert was the last child of a close-knit family. They
might not have had much in material possessions, but they
were millionaires in love. While Robert spoke English flu-
ently, his non-English-speaking family came many times to
admire his work, to smile at me and shake my hand, always
with a goodbye hug. They seemed to appreciate my efforts at
broken Spanish. I relished the interest his older sister showed
in Robert's accomplishments by her frequent visits. Her children spotted him immediately in the classroom and ran to
Robert. His hugs and kisses for them melted my heart.

At the end of the first day of school, I found my first "I love you" note from Robert. Before the school year ended, I had 180 notes from him, a love note each day. I still have them. Robert's superior work and creativity, especially in art, told me volumes about his future. I was approaching retirement, and it was my greatest year. I loved the children more than ever and they seemed to learn more than ever.

Before I knew it, the school year had ended. "This is for you Mrs. Clayton. I will miss you. I love you." Robert handed me a used Barbie doll with a make-do dress of red and yellow crepe paper. It stood in a glass vase. Red ribbons around the glass held two tiny hearts. One heart read "Robert," the other "Mrs. Clayton." Did Robert have to sacrifice something he loved to give me this gift? Could he have traded something he treasured with another sibling? Holding back my tears was not an option.

His family also came to tell me goodbye. Robert's dad hugged me and handed me an envelope. Inside it was a one-dollar bill with a note: "*Un regalo para ti con muchas gracias para ensenar nos hijito.*" (A present for you with many thanks for teaching our little son.) This time the tears burst into a river. With a widow's mite and a heart of love, I had received the gift of all gifts. I still have the dollar and will keep it always. Robert's parents had supported me all year at parent conferences, parties, and other activities. We had become close friends as we laughed at my Spanish with a southern accent. Robert left me with a piece of his heart.

The next year I received many phone calls from Robert. "Mrs. Clayton, this is Robert. I just wanted to tell you, I . . . uh . . . well, I . . . uh, I just want to say Mrs. Clayton, I just want to say, well . . . I just want to say 'I love you.'"

As a third grader Robert called and invited me to an art show. His work had won first prize. I beamed with pride as he showed me his work.

In sixth grade, Robert invited me to his class graduation. He made a beautiful speech. He immediately came down the steps to hug his family and me. I cried.

Robert's phone calls were not as frequent after that, and I understood completely. He was growing up, and I was thrilled upon reading his many accomplishments in our local newspaper.

One day in late May I received a phone call. "Mrs. Clayton, I love you." I recognized the voice immediately. "This is Robert. Remember me? I was in your class the year you retired."

"Well, thank you, Robert. After ten years you still remember me?"

"I could never forget you. Mrs. Clayton. I'm calling to see if you could come to my high school graduation. It's Saturday afternoon at one o'clock."

"Of course, my husband and I will be there, and thank you so much!"

On the drive, I told Emmitt about all the wonderful things I remembered about Robert and his family. Imagine my excitement when I saw Robert's name as valedictorian on the program. I had always known his potential.

Robert gave a marvelous valedictory address. He told of wonderful heights to be achieved, persistence for seeking the good, and the determination to never give up. My pride in him could not be measured. He then gave his speech in beautiful Spanish.

After that I heard Robert saying, "Now I want to honor a person who has had a profound effect upon my life. She set me on a path in second grade, leading me to success." He reached under the podium and pulled out a big cuddly brown teddy bear. "Mrs. Clayton, this is for you."

I totally lost it! Tears dropped on everyone. Robert walked down the steps and walked toward me in the audience, holding out the teddy bear to me. I literally ran to meet him, crying all the way. He cried too and we hugged a long time while the audience clapped.

After the ceremony, Robert's dad walked up with a bouquet of yellow carnations and a card written in Spanish. With tears in his eyes he hugged me. He kept repeating, "*Gracias hermosa maestra!"* While I couldn't keep up with all the Spanish, his body language and his eyes spoke volumes of love.

At home I opened my beautiful cards. I read them ever so slowly and savored every word. There was one from Robert's dad, which translated said: *"In the most painful fights of life, when so much crookedness is around us and we cry, there is one love who will always love you, and one that will never forget you."*

There was one from Robert's mom: *"You showed him how to read, you showed him how to sing, and you showed him how to succeed. In this day I dedicate and send one kiss from a loveable child who loves you."*

I lost contact with Robert for a time, but as usual, I prayed for him as I did all of my students. I didn't know where they all were, but God did.

It had been seven years since Robert's high school graduation, but the other day the doorbell rang.

"Robert, I'm so glad to see you!"

My husband hugged him too and we all sat down to catch up on his life. Before leaving he handed me an invitation to his college graduation. As he handed it to me, he said, "I always knew you prayed for me and all of your students, but I wondered if you ever saw the effects of your prayers. I wanted to tell you I am one of those unexpected prayers."

I have to be the happiest retired teacher in the world. Robert gave me a child's heart and that is a heart that lasts forever!

⌇⌇

Joan Clayton is a passionate writer from Portales, New Mexico. Her early pupil, Robert, went to Eastern New Mexico University all four years with a scholarship every year, majoring in electronics. Joan has written nine books and has written ten stories for various Chicken Soup for the Soul *publications. She also has many stories in various anthologies. She and her husband, Emmitt, attend Third & Kilgore Church of Christ in Portales. Her website is www.joanclayton.com.*

37

Revised Life

Joanne Lehman

∞

Ipick up another capstone essay to grade. In this assignment, my English composition students tell me what they've learned about writing. Brittany (all names changed) writes: "My exquisite instructor has taught me the craft of writing through her personal stories and passionate writing skills. I am so thankful and blessed that she was my professor." *Me, "exquisite," really?* I smile at the thought of Brittany—white leggings and pink cowboy boots—telling the class she always drinks hot cocoa when she writes.

I move on to Alyssa's paper. Yesterday after class Alyssa returned to the room. "Mrs. Lehman, I never talked to you, but . . ." I felt a twinge of anxiety. *Had I forgotten to return a paper? Was she going to question a grade?* "Would it be okay if I pray with you?" she asked. Near the door of the classroom my student earnestly prayed for my health, energy, family, and my life—which she described as "a vapor." Afterward, we chatted for a few minutes about faith, writing, and life.

Then there was Henry, a bit older than the other students, a military veteran who had grown up in a foster home. He didn't like writing and left the textbook in a car he sold. I loaned him a book. Henry often missed class or came in late, so I reported him to the student retention office. After this, he apologized and started wearing a sport coat and tie. He came to the writing center and we worked on his papers. On the last day of class he thanked me for helping him. We didn't mention the textbook.

This is my fourth year of teaching composition and literature after a lifetime of preparation. At this same school, I experienced grace as a student myself. Now I extend it to others. Reading their essays, I'm humbled and amazed at what they've already experienced. At times, I'm frustrated with their lack of motivation, attitude problems, and immaturity. I tire of their distracting and ever-present cell phones. When I get their attention, I talk to them about writing and share my passion for the craft, the art. I teach them to combine choppy Twitter sentences, and to repair fractured syntax. We solve the mystery of commas and semicolons and say goodbye to the five-paragraph essay. I tell them to write about their lives and things that matter to them. And we revise, revise, and revise again.

My students know I revise my own writing. What they don't know is that with God's help I also revised my life. Sitting in the empty classroom after Brittany, Alyssa, Henry, and the rest have gone, I think back to my student years at Malone. I was a returned college dropout slowly earning credits. Each semester I met briefly with the Communication Arts department chair to register for the next term. "You still don't have a math credit" she reminded me every time. I avoided her eyes and gazed at the poster on her wall—an empty Adirondack chair, vaporous skies, and not much else.

I envied my advisor, several years my junior. I wanted her friendship but she kept things professional. Despite my age—over forty—I still had a lot of growing up to do. I was insecure and passive, afraid to ask for what I needed. I didn't believe I belonged in the desk I sat in or the groups that formed after class. I couldn't look at a math book. My fragmented life as wife, mother, student, and employee made me chronically anxious.

"I'm going to refer you to the counseling office. Maybe they can help you with the questions you have about completing these math courses," my advisor said. She looked over my schedule, signed her name, and dismissively handed me the referral. I stood and faced the poster of the empty chair, then turned my back on it and left. That picture was a metaphor, but one I couldn't grasp.

I told the counselor I had a disability and needed to be excused from the course. We talked about my life, my aspirations, my anxieties, and eventually about math. We sat in a tiny office with a small round table between us. My guide took a legal pad and drew a crude picture of a wall—a barrier labeled MATH. "You're over here," he said, drawing a stick figure. "Graduation and your diploma are here." His rectangle could have been a mortarboard or a diploma. "There is only one way from where you are now to here" he said. "You have to go *through* this wall. There is no way around it." His pen traced the course for me. I left, angry and overwhelmed. Driving onto the expressway, tears of frustration welled up. *I don't need a degree to be happy. I don't need a diploma. Writers don't need diplomas to write.* But these were just more lies I told myself.

In the end I did the work—with God's grace and the support of many others. I became a community relations specialist and used the skills I'd gained in my (unfinished) degree program. My employer encouraged me to earn the degree and adjusted my schedule so I could attend early morning classes. I got a tutor. Nine years from when I returned to college, I graduated.

My job kept me busy, but there was still time to write poetry. I wrote a newspaper column and press releases. I attended writers' workshops and eventually won an important poetry prize. I organized events that fed my passion for writing and started a writers' group. Ten years later, I was still writing, still revising, and still imagining myself as an English teacher. I enrolled in a creative writing program and completed the degree in two short years. Soon afterward, I got a call from Malone University, where the motto is "Christ's Kingdom First." The verse from Jeremiah 29:11 on my graduation program in 1996 was prophetic: "For I know the plans I have for you, says the Lord, plans to prosper you and not to harm you. Plans to give you hope and a future" (NIV).

Now, sometimes in Founder's Hall, I catch the scent a school building holds in its walls for decades—is it an air freshener, a cleaning agent, or some long-time employee's lingering cologne? Who knows? When I walk down that hall, I remember my earlier years at Malone and thank God for helping me revise my life.

Students with attitude problems? I had one too. An older student who doesn't quite fit? That was me. Someone who "hates to write" or has a "learning disability"? I get it. *This is that future*, I think as I grade another capstone essay. If a student writes that I'm "exquisite," I might argue with her word choice or imagine she is fishing for a better grade. Or, I might accept her unique phrasing as God's wild blessing, the fullness of that empty chair, my life—this grace-filled "vapor."

∞

Joanne Lehman teaches writing and literature at Malone University. She has a BA in communication arts from Malone College (Canton, Ohio) and earned a master's of fine arts from Ashland University in 2009. Joanne's poetry has appeared in Artful Dodge, Great River Review, Windhover, Dreamseeker, Rejoice!, The Mennonite, *and other publications. She is the author of* Kairos: A Novel *and*

Traces of Treasure: Quest for God in the Commonplace, *both published by Herald Press. She won the 2004 Wick Poetry Prize for her chapbook* Morning Song. *Her chapbook* Driving in the Fog *is scheduled for release in April 2013. Joanne lives with her husband, Ralph, in Apple Creek, Ohio. They have two children, Laura Lehman Amstutz (Virginia) and Jeremy Lehman (Ohio), and four grandchildren.*

Enough

38

A Walk with My Son

Jodi Nisly Hertzler

⬯

Perhaps it was the chilly, drizzly morning (a drastic change from the muggy, sunny July weather we'd endured all week). Perhaps it was awakening too late to claim the favored corner of the couch. Or perhaps it was the fact that his younger brother had already selected the Saturday cartoon to be watched that morning. Whatever it was, my son was having a horrible morning. And things only worsened when an art project he'd labored over the last twenty-four hours disintegrated during the final steps. My husband and I winced at the shrieks of despair and anguish emitting from his bedroom. Flinched as he shouted at his brother to go away. Nearly fled the house as he stormed back downstairs, clearly caught between tears and the urge to break every window in the house.

Every attempt to defuse the situation resulted in bellowed disagreement. We tried to engage his help with the family jigsaw puzzle, then had to send him away for fear of injury to the puzzle or to his siblings. I attempted to provide a comfortable place for him to read in solitude, but his funk had robbed him of the ability to concentrate. Food didn't help; timeouts didn't help.

I was tempted to leave the boy to stew in his own angry juices. He was clearly ruining everyone's relaxed Saturday morning with his eleven-year-old angst, and I honestly didn't feel like dealing with such a maelstrom of emotion. I poured myself a cup of coffee and prepared to just wait it out. But watching him, I was reminded of myself at his age, and I recalled the volatile mood swings I used to have; I saw myself in that angry boy huddled on the couch, growling at anyone who glanced his way. And I remembered my father's method of dealing with me. When he'd see me caught up in my emotions—all tangled up in anger and frustration with no tools to free myself—my gentle, patient father would insist that we go for a walk. I have many memories of twilight walks around our neighborhood, talking with my dad, the air and exercise and company easing my troubled mind.

So I took a fortifying gulp of coffee and a deep breath and gingerly approached the seething dragon that lay within my son. "How about we go for a walk?"

I was sure he'd say no. The cold, wet drizzle outside was hardly inviting. But perhaps the miserable weather appealed to his inner tempest, because he agreed at once. So we set out. I wasn't sure what to expect. I told myself not to bring up the morning's troubles, but to allow him to dictate the level of interaction. We jogged to the intersection, crossed the busy highway, and progressed up the sidewalk, toward a small woodland not far away.

The rain-washed air and burst of exercise must have had a purging effect, because the treetops of our destination were barely in sight when my son started unloading. He took me step by step through his failed attempt at art. But his voice remained calm; he didn't dissolve into tears or anger. I expressed my understanding. We considered options for repair. He sighed.

Then we moved on to other topics. We talked about the upcoming school year, and he admitted to nervousness about how much harder things will be in middle school. I agreed that the work might be more difficult but assured him that he's a quick learner and that his main challenge will be organization. He considered that for a moment, then challenged me to a race to the edge of the woods. He won (barely).

We entered the woods, and the conversation turned to observations of the fallout from a recent violent windstorm. We marveled over felled trees and the park bench that lay splintered under one of them. We looked for poison ivy and studied stream levels. We breathed clean, fresh air and admired the umbrella of trees sheltering us from the rain. We traversed muddy paths, jumped over puddles, and gingerly made our way across a wooden plank, wondering at the fate of the bridge that once lived there.

As we walked, I watched my son. My firstborn. This boy on the cusp of puberty. He's small for his age, but he's quick and strong and agile. And barefoot—even on hikes, my boy disdains shoes. Large hazel eyes belie the workings of a mischievous mind and remind me of his first year, when old ladies in grocery stores used to coo, "Hello, bright eyes" when they saw him. His persistent curiosity about the world is the reason we had to buy toilet locks when he was a toddler. He struggles to concentrate in school, but he's an amazingly creative thinker and constantly surprises me with the things he comes up with. Of all my children, he's the one who most often causes me to lose my temper, but he's also the one who most often makes me laugh.

I pondered these things as we walked back home, and I acknowledged that we're approaching a turning point. My boy is nearing the end of his boyhood. Male hormones will soon take over and change him into someone I can't quite imagine yet. I have high hopes for the man he'll become, but I already mourn the loss of the tree-climbing, Lego-building, creek-exploring child he is.

Months have passed since that day. My son still reminisces about that walk we took in the rain, but for me it's more than a fun memory. It was a moment out of time. This walk that we took—the rain that chilled our cheeks and washed our ragged emotions, the trees that provided a sheltering canopy over us—did more than just calm an angry eleven-year-old. It helped me to put our present preteen frustrations into the perspective of the entire life path that my son is journeying, from his first breaths in my arms to the first time I watched him climb aboard a school bus, and on into the misty, unknowable future. I was granted a new connection to my son right at the time when he's starting to become his own man.

That morning walk gave us time to think and to talk and to play together. A chilly, drizzly, wonderful space in time.

Jodi Nisly Hertzler is a tutor at Eastern Mennonite School, proofreader and copy editor for MennoMedia, the author of Ask Third Way Café: 50 Common and Quirky Questions About Mennonites, *and a guest columnist for the* Another Way *newspaper column. She and her husband, Shelby, have two sons and one daughter. They are members of Community Mennonite Church in Harrisonburg, Virginia.*

39

The Smell of Grace

Karen Andres

∽

I sat on a wooden beam, poking a stick at the ground and wondering what it was I was seeking. The events of the previous months were still reeling in my head and had motivated me to seclude myself in a place where I knew no one. This was amazing, considering that I am an introvert and seeking new people and places is not an easy task.

Even more amazing to those who know me was that I drove by myself to another state, to a place I had never been before. I have a reputation for easily getting lost even a few miles from home. But this situation called for drastic measures on my part. My fears of getting lost or meeting new people did not even matter to me anymore. I needed to find out how to deal with the deep sadness within.

Why I was sad was no mystery. A beautiful, forty-nine-year-old woman from my congregation had taken her own life. As one of the pastors who had walked with her for nine years, I was stunned. Oh, I had learned a lot about issues regarding abuse and mental illness just by listening to her stories. I knew in my head I could not take responsibility for her actions. There were so many others who tried to help her; professional counseling had been a part of her life for more than twenty years. Still, my heart was aching and I could not put my finger on the core of my emptiness. I felt there was something I had lost and I could not get it back.

So, here I was at a Catholic retreat center in the hills of Iowa. This was an eight-day silent retreat. Talking was allowed only one hour a day with a spiritual director and at mass. One would think that, for an introvert, being silent for eight days would be a relief. I certainly enjoyed not having to come up with clever conversation at mealtime with the other participants.

However, silence can be very revealing, even frightening. On the third day of meeting with a spiritual director, I sensed a bit of frustration on her part. She was not happy that we had not had a "breakthrough" moment. She was actually in training to be a director, and I couldn't help but think that she was hoping for some miraculous thing to happen so that she could report to her instructor how successful it had been. But we still had five days to go. I was getting impatient myself, but I knew from experience that the Spirit sometimes moves slower than I would like.

So, here I sat on a wooden beam out in the grassy area watching the ants move on the ground. I remember thinking to myself that the ants knew more than I did at that point. They at least knew how to navigate and gather food. I was clueless as to what I needed. So I decided to pray honestly.

"Lord, I admit I am clueless. I know why I'm here but I don't know how to find healing for my inner being. I don't know if I feel connected to you right now. I feel like I'm missing something. Please help me."

Then, bored with the ants, I got up and headed for a small wooded area that seemed inviting at the time. As I got closer, I smelled the obnoxious smell of a skunk. "I'm not going near that area," I concluded. I sat back down on the beam.

Then, in my heart voice I heard these words: "Do you believe I can protect you from a skunk?" I raised my head as if someone had spoken to me directly.

"What?" I replied as if someone would answer. And then those words came again,

"Do you believe I can protect you from a skunk?"

Okay, I thought, *I don't know if this is God speaking but what do I have to lose? I am here to find healing so I am going to take a chance.* "Yes, of course, you are God," I replied with some cynicism in my voice. "You can do anything."

Then, a quick response came as if someone was truly standing there. I heard these words of invitation, "Go back into the woods."

Feeling a bit guarded at this point, I replied, "Excuse me, but why would I put myself in harm's way intentionally?"

Again, the invitation, "Go back into the woods."

Well, by now I really thought I had nothing to lose. I came to find healing, and if this was God speaking to me, I was going to "test the Spirit" and see what miraculous thing could happen. So I proceeded to walk slowly toward the wooded area again, rather cautiously as the skunk smell began to simmer in my nostrils. Slowly and gently I sat down on a stump for a time and all became still. I looked around and saw no sign of a skunk. Suddenly the morning sunlight peered through the trees and it seemed as though it focused right on my being. I felt warmth and peace even in that crisp morning air, and tears began to stream down my cheeks as if some strange love overpowered me. This time words of assurance came to me, "See, you haven't lost your faith. You still trust in me. My love and grace is enough for you." So that was it. I thought I had lost my faith. The flood waters let loose as it was finally revealed to me what I was missing.

Every day at mass at the retreat center we had sung these words, "Give me nothing more than your love and grace. These alone, O God, are enough for me." These words have stuck with me as words to live by. Grace was offered as a free gift and was put into motion when I was open to receive it.

I made a spiritual director very happy that day. And then, as if the skunk event wasn't enough, God provided me with a dream later that week of the woman who died. Being an avid runner, she was running in the dream, but this time she was running with a smile on her face and toward a wonderful place. Not everyone finds healing on this side of heaven, but could it be that God's healing presence continues to follow us through eternity! I am counting on it—the wonderful smell of grace!

∞

Karen Andres completed ten years in December 2012 as associate pastor at Tabor Mennonite Church, Newton, Kansas, and is now a part-time chaplain at Prairie View Mental Health Center in Newton. She is currently in the graduate program at Emporia State University in mental health counseling. She is a spiritual director, receiving training from Associated Mennonite Biblical Seminary. She also teaches courses in the Spiritual Strengths Cancer Care Program administered by the Congregation of the Sisters of St. Joseph in Wichita, Kansas. She is married to David Andres, a farmer, and has one son and one soon-to-be daughter-in-law. She enjoys quilting, music, and loves animals.

40

A Walk with God

Carrie Martens

∞

My experience of prayer had been entirely word-based all my life. I had been taught to consider prayer as a conversation. We articulated our thoughts, desires, laments to God with our analytical minds, with our words, and perhaps we also listened, though for what I was never entirely sure. To some small degree I did connect with God through these prayers, yet I was always left feeling like something was missing—that somehow in the process of communing with God there should be more. More love, more interaction, more connection, more grace.

And then my spiritual director, Linda Lehman Thomas, taught me that I could pray with my imagination. At that point my spiritual world blossomed. It was like I had been sitting with God in a dark room and suddenly someone told me that I could turn on the light. Prayer for me is still a conversation at times, but it is also so much more. I'm a visual person with a vivid imagination and to discover that God was willing to meet me in that space touched me deeply. I will share it in detail here as an example of how this kind of prayer works, for you to try if you feel so led.

One of my first and most dynamic experiences of praying imaginatively surprised me in part because I came to the encounter with few expectations. Sitting in my room, I was prepared to experiment with this type of prayer, prepared to do my part but honestly not prepared to meet God in any profound way.

Sitting quietly I closed my eyes and slowed my breathing. I allowed myself to enter into my inner world, to use my inner senses, setting aside the sounds and sights of the outer world. I found myself in an empty space with a door. Hesitantly, I opened the door and crossed the threshold into a meadow. And perhaps this next part sounds bizarre, or maybe cliché, but I found Jesus sitting there on a rock, waiting. Waiting for me to come to him. And so I did. I approached him, and he held out his hand. It was warm and gentle. It was safe. The space I was in felt infinitely safe. And I'm sure I spoke to him, though I can no longer recall what I might have said. And he spoke to me. He told me that he wanted to show me something and asked me to walk with him. A simple invitation to walk with God.

And we walked. We walked through the grass beneath the brilliant blue sky and gradually the landscape changed. The landscape that lay before me when we stopped walking is forever etched in my mind. When we stopped we were standing in the sand. Before me was the most expansive sky, the clearest water, the brightest sun, and a series of curious rock formations partially immersed by the tide. Jesus led me through the shallow water as it lapped over our feet. We approached the rock formations and Jesus began to explain to me how they were created, the way the water constantly washed over the rocks, the erosion that impacted their form over the years. He took my hand and placed it on the cool surface of the rock, and together we ran our fingers over the places worn smooth and the rough edges that had yet to be altered. I have no idea how

long we spent standing there together exploring the surface
of that rock, marveling at the variations of color and tex-
ture, contemplating the massive, yet infinitely slow changes
that had taken place in this small corner of creation. But at
some point, as I stood there with my hand on the side of
this large rock, Jesus covered my hand with his and he told
me that I am like that rock, that we are all like that rock.
Even though there are days when we feel that we are not
growing and changing, even though there are days when
we feel stuck, the process is always at work. The waters of
life continue to flow over us, gently smoothing our rough
edges, shaping us into the people we were created to be.
And that was the message I needed most that day, that day
when I felt stuck and incredibly frustrated, when I felt like I
had repeated the same pattern and made the same mistake
yet again. I needed to know that change was happening,
no matter how slow, and that those changes are profound.

As we began to walk away from the rock, I felt a sense
of awe, a sense of mystery, a sense of divine connection,
and a sense of panic. Surely in that moment the appropriate
response to God would be worship, some kind of expression
of praise or gratitude. I wracked my brain for ideas: what
would be right, how did one express gratitude in one's imagination when standing on the beach with Jesus. I had no feeling for how to proceed in such a situation! And then, sensing
my panic, Jesus stopped me and turned me toward him. As I
blurted out my confused thoughts, he smiled. He told me that
this was not the time to concern myself with proper worship.
He just looked at me and said, "Let me wash your feet." He
led me to a small pool that had gathered in the midst of some
low rocks and gestured for me to sit. Jesus, the Christ, the one
whom I had always been taught to worship, began to gently
scoop the cool clear water over my sandy feet, washing away
any sense of inadequacy and cleansing me with his grace.

And I wept. Never in my life had I felt so loved, never in
my life had I felt that I was so completely sufficient. In that
moment, grace was enough.

∽

Carrie Martens is a 2011 graduate of Associated Mennonite Biblical Seminary. Prior to attending AMBS she completed a BA at Canadian Mennonite University. Carrie's passion for ministry lies in the area of Christian formation, specifically engaging children of all ages as they seek to encounter God through the biblical story, prayer, and rituals. Some of the most life-giving experiences in Carrie's work have been parent/child prayer classes, teaching Sunday school, leading children's prayer retreats, and providing individual spiritual guidance for children and youth. Carrie currently resides in Winnipeg, Manitoba, and is exploring where God might be calling her to use her gifts.

41

The Grace of Enough

Sherah-Leigh Gerber

∽

It's amazing how useless a car can be with a flat tire, smashed-in driver door, cracked windows, and a contorted wheelbase. The crash happened in an instant, yet the guilt I felt lasted much longer.

I couldn't forgive myself for my own carelessness. Not only did the accident dramatically change the end to what had been a fun weekend trip with a girlfriend, it also required my in-laws to change plans and come retrieve me (and tow the car) more than four hundred miles. Thankfully it only involved my car and a large flashing construction sign, and neither my passenger nor I were injured. However, as I surveyed the heap of metal that had been my car, I was quite distraught. Even with insurance to replace the car, the money we had been carefully, painfully saving for the next phase of life had to be used.

"It's only money. It's only a car." People tried to cheer me.

"At least you are fine," they would say. "That's what your savings are for."

As I repeated these unhelpful comments over a cup of coffee with my best friend, it dawned on me that in my way of thinking and behaving there would never be "enough." If I insisted on using this type of framework for measuring contentment in my life, I was chasing an elusive dream.

How could I say that having my health, my life wasn't "enough"? God's grace had provided enough—enough to cover the damages, enough to grant me another day of life, enough to humbly accept help from others.

I received this gift of grace four years ago, and it has changed my life. My first (and thankfully only) car accident not only destroyed my car, but it also broke through the web of lies and false ideals that I was using to rate success and define contentment.

As I reflected on my life, I realized that before the car it had been the job. At the beginning of the year of the accident, my husband and I had moved to a small town so that he could join his family's business. My newly minted master's of divinity degree didn't find immediate translation in the rural community. Where could I find work that would be fulfilling?

I lamented and worried. In my humanness, I tried to shove pieces together. But it was God who provided, abundantly more than I could have imagined for myself, a gift of grace—a job that used my gifts and training, a job that was flexible and life giving.

Once I had the job I enjoyed, I immediately thought about starting a family. There wasn't time to rest in the contentment of a goal achieved or a dream satisfied. It wasn't "enough." Then I had the accident. God gave me this beautiful gift—the grace of enough.

However, a few months later, I realized that this precious gift of grace had been shoved to the back of the shelf once again. After what felt like a long struggle with fertility, when I finally got over the joyous shock of positive news, being pregnant ended up not being enough either.

When the doctor said this may not be a viable pregnancy, the amazing, joyous high I had just experienced was ripped away and I sunk to new depths. It was on that drive home from the doctor's office that I realized that, despite my prayers, being pregnant wasn't enough either.

And then, in a flash of insight, I realized that even if I birthed a healthy child, it would still not be "enough." Parenting brings a new set of worries, feelings of anxiety and inadequacy, more fears, more demands on an already full life. Thankfully, the grace of enough was a package that I could reopen—a gift I could experience and accept again.

The reality I live with is that there is no amount of money that I can save that will be enough to clean up any potential disaster. There isn't "enough" to buy back someone's health, to restore broken relationships, to heal the pain of loss.

Incorporating the gift of enough into the rhythms of my daily life has come at a providential time. I am now anticipating the arrival of our second child. It has been a challenging pregnancy, and it's easy to become fearful about the transitions that accompany adding a new family member. I know the intensity of my life is about to increase yet again, and I will be searching for a new balance—enough time for the many important people and tasks.

I begin to get overwhelmed, but then I take a deep breath and remember the gift of grace I have received (and must claim daily); having enough means I embrace the opportunity to live today. "Enough" is when my daily need is met and I can face the challenges of tomorrow with hope, faith, and trust that yet again God will provide.

Just as God is faithful, God is also a God of abundance. God is radically prodigal—recklessly lavish and generous. For me to live into this truth, to accept this gift of grace, means rejecting the cultural lie of scarcity. It means quieting the voices of doubt and insecurity to make space for the still small voice.

This same gift of grace that has been manifest powerfully in my life is available to all. Do you hear God's whispering in your own heart?

"Dear Child, I am enough.
There is enough.
I am Jehovah Jireh.
I am your Provider."

Will you quiet yourself to hear? Will you be still and receive? Will you accept the gift of the grace of enough in your life?

∞

Sherah-Leigh (Zehr) Gerber works part time as coordinator of volunteers for Ohio Conference of Mennonite Church USA. A graduate of Eastern Mennonite University (BA) and Eastern Mennonite Seminary (MDiv), she has served in a variety of pastoral roles and written curriculum. Sherah-Leigh enjoys reading, baking, or a having a cup of coffee with friends in her spare time. She lives with her husband and their two young children in Kidron, Ohio, where they are active members of Kidron Mennonite Church.

Support

42

Mercy at the Library

Jennifer Delanty

∽

Before I started school, I wondered what my sister meant when she would say, "I wanna go to the li-berry." My mind pictured her lying down while eating ripe strawberries. That did seem pretty special.

I don't remember the first time I actually went to the library, but that word contained something far greater than the picture my mind had made. Libraries were countless shelves of books, and books were very fun and interesting—worlds made out of words! I also loved the refuge of quiet and calm the library provided, away from the complications at home that I could not resolve.

My favorite books to check out from the school library were written by Lois Lenski, about children living in different regions across our nation. The pioneer life of Laura Ingalls Wilder also captivated me.

The twentieth century in which I was living was very different from Laura's; divorce was a topic her books did not cover. Our parents' 1970 divorce left my two siblings and me unsupervised after school until our mother arrived home from work with our baby brother in tow. We didn't know anyone else at school whose parents were divorced, so we kept quiet about our sea of change.

To my delight, sometimes after school, my third grade teacher would take me in her Volkswagen bus to the downtown public library. It was enormous compared to our school library. I applied for my very own manila cardboard library card. My teacher promptly returned the books on a timely basis so I wouldn't be assessed any fines.

In 1972, we moved across the river to the west side of the city, away from my generous teacher and all we had known. It was a difficult transition. Our new home was tiny in the unfamiliar neighborhood. The small park nearby was ruled by an angry girl. Screaming like a banshee, she would run out anyone who tried to come and play. When I started fifth grade as the new girl, I was wary of her and everyone else. That first day when no one knew my name, I was surprised to hear "Hello, Jennifer" when I entered the school library. The librarian from my former school had transferred to my new elementary school, and I was flooded with relief to see a familiar, friendly face. Once again, the library was my refuge. Daily, I would check out a book, read it that evening, and return it the following day for another. Other students labeled me "weird" for reading so much.

The west branch of the city library was another saving grace and within walking distance from our new home. The children's section on the second floor was cozy and quiet. I perched next to the window like a cat, tucked away in my newfound refuge. One day I found a book about a South African girl named Nomusa. We had learned about her culture and continent during fourth grade at my old school. I eagerly checked out this book since it was not the same one we had used in our studies. I was so happy that I would get to read more about Nomusa.

When it was time to return the book, I could not find it anywhere. It wasn't in my classroom desk, nor did I find it in my dad's apartment during my next visit. No matter how many times I went through our bookshelves and my bedroom, it was not to be found. I knew I couldn't check out any more books with this one unreturned.

This wonderful branch library was the only thing I liked about moving across town. But now, only a few months later, I could no longer return. I was too embarrassed and ashamed to admit to the librarian that the book was lost and a two-cent daily fine was accumulating. I had no money for fines or the cost of replacing the book. Confessing this to my mother was out of the question; her own worries were far more grave. So, like that angry girl who prevented access to the park, I prevented myself access to the branch library. I even started to resent Nomusa for beguiling me to check out that book in the first place.

I had so many losses at that point in my life that losing access to this branch library was comparatively inconsequential. Recalling it now, I recognize it as a loss of innocence, another removal of a refuge from the anger, violence, and abuse that were ugly constants in our home.

About a year later, I found the Nomusa book stuck between the wall and my bunk bed. What a relief! I went straight to the library, but could not show the long-lost book to the librarian. I probably owed more fines than the book was worth, and I had no money anyway. My mother would have a fit if she knew I owed a fine like that. I dropped the book in the return slot and slunk away to continue my self-imposed exile.

Another year went by, and a junior high school assignment compelled me again to use the west branch library. I stood before the librarian with a stack of source books while she retrieved my dreaded fine list. Fear clutched my heart while I wondered how much I owed. I chastised myself for not facing the consequences when I returned the Nomusa book; I really needed these books for my assignment. I braced myself for certain recrimination.

But as the librarian reviewed the accumulation noted on the card, she muttered, "Oh, this is so old, I'm not even going to worry about it." She tore up my fine card and processed my stack of books. My debt was cleared. I was thunderstruck!

Life up to that point had been conditional. Love and acceptance were not the norm in our family; guilty was the presumed verdict whenever anything was amiss. Mistakes did not deserve forgiveness. On that day, though, a librarian gave me a glimpse that perhaps life could be different from what I had experienced as a dreadful scorecard of transgressions, similar to that fine list. Dismissing my debt was an act of grace and mercy. Such unearned kindness was unfamiliar outside my known world. At that point, I did not know unconditional love existed, but I was moving inexorably toward it.

Ironically, or perhaps appropriately, the Ndebele name Nomusa means "merciful." A lost book and merciful librarian helped me gain a glimmering of the more bountiful life that God was holding in store. Turning toward Jesus Christ a few years later would enable greater grace and mercy than the refuge the library had been to me as a young child. Just as the library revealed new horizons and vistas when I was very young, the Mennonite denomination I claimed offered me an entirely new way of living and being, into a different and better world, built with kindness and peace. 'Tis a beautiful, grace-filled place from which I cannot and will not be exiled. Thanks be to God.

∽

Jennifer Delanty attends Seattle Mennonite Church and is living happily ever after.

43

Grace on Venomous Mountain

Michelle Sinclair

∞

Cold mountaintop wind roared in my ears. The path through the snow had vanished, along with visibility beyond forty feet. I had no map, no compass, and no idea where the two-thousand-foot cliffs I was supposed to be avoiding were lurking.

My sister Doreen had gone to Scotland for her study abroad experience, and I went to visit her on her spring break. We thought it would be cool to hike Ben Nevis, the 4,409-foot highest peak in the British Isles. We figured it would be a bit of a trek, but we enjoy hiking, and Scotland's not Nepal, right?

Without doing any real research, I learned Ben Nevis is the most popular Munro—the elite club of Scottish peaks higher than three thousand feet—and attracts a wide variety of goers. The website (www.undiscoveredscotland.co.uk) claims the round trip takes five hours for experienced "Munro baggers." That's about eight hours for the rest of us.

Our solution? Leave early in the morning and take our time. I read somewhere that it could be dangerous, but so long as we stuck to the trail, I figured we'd survive. That was supposed to be a figure of speech.

We checked into a hikers' hostel in the nearby town of Fort William, where a staff member took one look at us and handed us a Ben Nevis survival pamphlet. We barely skimmed it, figuring this was just one of those overly cautious things they had to do to avoid being sued. But this was Scotland, not the United States, and even though you don't need oxygen tanks or belaying experience to reach the summit, its seemingly mild nature and the cliffs on three sides are what make the *Beinn Nibheis*, or "Venomous Mountain," so dangerous.

On a brisk April morning, we set out at eight o'clock in jeans, tennis shoes (her), and cheap hiking boots (me). We enjoyed the scenery and the gradual climb. Grazing sheep probably laughed at our huffing and puffing. Other hikers all seemed to have maps and serious mountain gear, and as we ascended higher, we began to have doubts. Very few trees dotted the scrubby brown landscape—an enormous change from the lush Appalachians I knew from home. Above our heads, the overcast sky hid the peak from view.

After a lunch of sandwiches, we had one banana left and less than a bottle of water. We entered the cloud, and as the valley below vanished, our world narrowed to an unstable path of rocks winding around the mountainside. To our surprise, we started seeing patches of snow. It went from being a novelty to a nuisance to an expanse of white with nothing to mark the trail but a row of footprints. At that point, the safe, smart choice would have been to turn back, but we had been hiking for four hours and I wanted my view. We pressed on until the footprints scattered—and with them our path.

Black rocks dotted the precipitous slope ahead. In the distance, gray fog and snow merged. Those cliffs had to be nearby. Some people with spiked trekking poles climbed straight up the steep hillside, while others walked to the right. But which was the safest route for two inexperienced hikers in jeans and tennis shoes?

Our careless pride had gotten us into this situation, but it certainly wasn't going to get us out of it. I tucked my proverbial tail between my legs and asked a friendly caravan of Irish hikers which way we should go. These angels in insulated pants didn't just point the way—they shared their trekking poles and welcomed us into their group. Of course they went straight up the incline, so with the help of the poles, we jammed our toes into the crusty surface and kept up the best we could.

The sharp wind drowned our voices. Bits of sky flashed through the wisps of clouds.

Then my heart beat hard as a low stone structure emerged through the distant fog. The summit! We'd made it!

Our mouths hanging open, we raced across the snow, fumbling in our coat pockets for our cameras. The cloud rushed overhead, unfurling the vista in maddeningly brief glimpses. We laughed with our heads tilted back, drinking in the day's first blue sky until—at last—the fog cleared the summit and completely rolled away. Thanks to our saviors of the day, we were granted grace to make it to the top.

I don't regret hiking Ben Nevis, but I do regret treating it like a Sunday afternoon hike. With the wealth of information at our fingertips, we had no excuse for going into an unfamiliar situation without doing proper research. Never again will I assume that warnings are just lawsuit avoidance and that I—in all my lofty self-reliance—can handle anything on my own.

But I'll still get out there to see God's creation in all its varied splendor, because for the rest of my life I will see those majestic glens and ridges of Scotland laid bare before my eyes. I will remember the feeling that followed, when the field of white poured across the sky below the peak, leaving me uncovered, higher than the clouds, higher than the other mountaintops jutting through the mist. Forget Everest or McKinley—I was on top of the world. And I was newly thankful for the grace to survive a hike for which I was unprepared.

Michelle D. Sinclair is an account executive in the advertising department of The Washington Post *and attends Northern Virginia Mennonite Church. She also writes monthly movie reviews for* Third Way Café's *(website)* Media Matters, *as well as guest columns for the* Another Way *newspaper column. In her spare time, she enjoys writing young adult novels, spending time with her husband, Brian, and playing with their cat, Josie.*

44

One More Time

Brenda Shelly

⌒⌒

My husband's mode of transportation continues to be a source of angst for me. Though at times it masquerades as a dependable station wagon, we at the Shelly house know the truth. At inconvenient and unpredictable intervals, the car just quits.

This could happen as Jim is just starting out or after he has driven several hundred miles. It does not distinguish between icy winter and the heat of summer. There is no rhyme or reason, but there's an annoying tendency to misbehave *just* as my longsuffering husband dares remark about an unusually long period of dependability.

It's been years with this same mystifying condition, a state which refuses to be diagnosed. When finally Jim's frustration swells, my tolerant spouse takes the maddening vehicle to the garage for repair. The mechanics attempt to replicate the disorder, but to no avail. Last month it received another unbelievable "clean bill of health." And driving home from the garage, the beast (affectionately called Lola by Jim and my magnanimous daughter) shut off once more.

The only silver lining in this annoying cloud of disrepair is that the car's episodes are fairly predictable in resolution. If one waits for the usual amount of time (approximately five minutes) the car will start up with a grin, as though woken from a nap, fully refreshed for the next two hundred miles.

And so it was, earlier this week, my husband phoned me from his office parking lot. The car refused to budge and having persisted in his usual twelve- or thirteen-hour workday, he was already late for supper. He thought he might just wait a few minutes and then start it up and be on his way. But Lola had again refused to come home, so Jim caught a ride with a coworker. Last night the scenario was similar. Only this time Lola let Jim get far enough from the office to be marooned at a nearby intersection. Predictably, dinner was again past due. While I was practicing my deep breathing, dear Jim was going to wait a little while and attempt to launch once more. A second call had him sounding a bit more peeved and he refused my offer to come and pick him up. He would decide what to do with his car (which was clogging the road) and call me back.

When next we spoke, he was fairly winded. This was the result of pushing and steering the annoying vehicle (by himself) to the driveway of the nearby Lowe's. And since Lola was now off the road (and Jim was exhausted from pushing hundreds of pounds in the heat and humidity), he agreed to a ride.

I arrived at the scene with an orange sign for the back of his car and a roll of scotch tape. The sign explained that the car had died and would be removed from the driveway by morning. Being a nurse I am usually happy to be the rescuer, so despite the second dry supper of the week, I was in pretty good spirits. In the meantime, Jim had spoken to a man in the garage at work. The man could not leave to attend the problem, but he did offer the use of a truck with which to tow the offending car back to the company garage. Though we were pressed for time, we dashed over to the garage to pick up the tow truck.

But when we got out of the tow truck Jim informed me that I would be "driving" his car . . . as in *steering and braking*, since the truck was not exactly equipped for towing and only had a rope to fasten between the truck and Lola.

"Do the brakes actually work when the car isn't running?" I asked. Jim's answer did nothing to cheer me. Expecting me to have no trouble *standing* on the brakes and yanking on the steering wheel while attempting *not* to hit the back of his company's truck, he seemed not worried in the least.

I decided I'd rather drive the tow truck as I did not want to be responsible for denting its back bumper. His response again was disheartening. "Well, it isn't really easy to *tow* something either. . . . and the truck does belong to the company." With a sense of impending doom and resignation, I climbed behind the wheel of Lola. Jim directed me to turn the key until the red lights lit. With a deep breath, I tried one more time to start her up before embarking on the crazy rope-pulling expedition to the garage. And she purred demurely like a cat waking from her nap. Stupid car.

Against my suggestion that we drive her to the garage and *leave* her there, Jim had already forgiven her trespasses and was happy to take her home with us.

He is a patient and merciful man. I know this because Lola and I have something in common. I too am a recurring recipient of grace. I'd like to insist that Jim sell Lola's disloyal carcass on eBay for parts, but forgiveness is a marvelous thing to watch and to receive. It is clear my husband and my heavenly Father have some similar tendencies as well. Okay, Lola. One more time.

∽

Brenda Shelly is a member of Blooming Glen Mennonite Church and school nurse at Penn View Christian School in Souderton, Pennsylvania. She is married to her high school sweetheart, Jim. They share two wonderful children, Isaac (25) of Harrisonburg, Virginia, and Aubrey (17) still at home in Hatfield, Pennsylvania. Writing anecdotes about finding God's faithfulness in everyday chaos brings Brenda a great deal of joy. You can find more of these tales by visiting her blog at pearlsinthepuddle.blogspot.com.

45

Consider It Sold

Ken Seitz

∞

Philip and Lois (Seitz) Kreider reside in Harrisonburg, Virginia. He worked nineteen years in the computer industry, pastored in Oregon, and has since served as an effective lay leader at their church in Virginia. Always the pastor, he has volunteered for many years as an industrial chaplain at a local industry. Lois has worked as a software trainer and office manager. Without children of their own, they have always taken an interest in nieces and nephews.

In April 2011, Philip and Lois were on a vacation trip to the West Coast and driving one morning somewhere in western Colorado. Suddenly Phil declared that they should begin to downsize their home. It was time in their life to get rid of possessions, including excess home furnishings and stuff in the basement and shop. While the topic had come up casually in prior conversations, this time Lois knew that Phil was utterly sincere. What were the inner stirrings? Why the sudden sense of urgency?

Together they recognized that over the years they had accumulated what now felt like a vast array of stuff, things eating away at their lives like a cancer. Add to that some mobility issues necessitating a home on one floor. And how do you sell a home in a depressed market to relocate to something smaller? But they felt strongly this was what God was asking of them, so they dared to put their home on the market in September 2011 and began a sustained and somewhat painful letting go.

Earlier they had happened on a sign at a nearby new housing development advertising reduced rates. Initial conversations with the developer went surprisingly well, offering what's known today in the industry as half a paired home at a price they could afford—contingent, of course, on selling their present property.

As 2011 morphed into 2012, the realtor arranged numerous showings of their home, but no offers materialized. Meanwhile, the new structure was on the drawing boards with the understanding that Phil would do a limited amount of the construction to reduce costs. The credit union came through with a loan to get the construction underway. While important aspects of the project were coming together wonderfully, month after month their other house sat unsold.

In May 2012, amidst all the uncertainty, Phil evidenced worrisome symptoms and several weeks later was diagnosed with colon cancer. Moreover, he needed radiation and chemotherapy to shrink the tumor in preparation for surgery later on. They wondered where that left them. How could Phil work on the house while getting heavy doses of cancer treatment? How could he help with the moving? Nevertheless, the two persevered with preparations for leaving their home of twenty-five years, all of which seemed futile so long as their home remained unsold. Concern mounted, for in addition to Phil's weakened condition, building expenses were piling up.

One day when he was out shopping, feeling alone and seemingly without options, Phil recalls praying in the restroom at Costco: "Lord, I do not know where to turn nor do I know what needs to be done next. Would you please help me understand your presence?"

Then, as he left the store to join Lois in the car, the unexpected happened. A phone call came from a close friend. The caller got right to the point. "Phil, have you sold your house?" When Phil said no, the friend at the other end responded, "Then consider it sold; have your realtor call me. Your job is to get well and to complete your downsizing by moving into your new home."

The realtor, when informed, exclaimed, "You have *some* friend!"

Phil submitted to the treatment routine and, in spite of feeling very unwell much of the time, struggled to accomplish his part of the construction on the new house, difficult as it was. On one such occasion, a neighbor stepped into the house one day while Phil was working there. She registered concern about the amount of physical effort Phil was exerting before she planted a supportive kiss on his cheek, a sample of the affectionate outpouring of many people, all of which helped him keep on. Meanwhile, Lois was home packing for the move, which occurred in August 2012.

Today, the two, with Jessie, their dog, are now at home in the new setting. There they reflect on the previous two years with wonder and gratitude. God's extravagant grace came through in many ways, but primarily in a friend's offer to purchase their previous home.

At the time of writing, the tumor has been removed surgically and is being followed up by a second round of six months of chemotherapy, hopefully to rid Phil's body of any residual cancer. Given the effects of the chemo cycles, he feels stronger some days than others. But if you visit with him and Lois, you will encounter a vibrant, hopeful spirit, very grateful for the way things unfolded so that the necessary downsizing was able to take place during a depressed housing market in the midst of dealing with the onset of cancer and follow-up treatment. And thanks to God's abundant grace working through a caring, compassionate friend who acted exactly at the moment of dire need.

∞

Ken Seitz began writing for Rejoice! *in 1993 while in church development work in Burlington, Vermont. Since then he has written for* Rejoice! *from Pennsylvania; California; Beirut, Lebanon; and now Harrisonburg, Virginia, where he and his wife, Audrey Metz, reside at Virginia Mennonite Retirement Community. Ken has been a pastor, service worker-administrator, and college teacher. He has lived in both Jerusalem and Beirut. He is a member of Park View Mennonite Church where he presently serves as congregational chair, sings in the church choir, and teaches an adult Sunday school class.*

Blessing

46

Amiroon

Ron Adams

∽

In 1981, I traveled to Calcutta, India, with a small group of seminarians to do evangelistic ministry. We gave that up pretty quickly, however.

Soon after we arrived, we met with an Indian Baptist pastor. He taught us some Indian history. He taught us a bit about Hinduism. But what has stayed with me all these years is one of the first things he said to us. He said that if we'd come to Calcutta thinking we were bringing Jesus with us, we should get back on the plane and go home. But, if we'd come to Calcutta seeking the Jesus already there, we should stay and see what we could see. We stayed and set about looking for Jesus.

We volunteered with Mother Teresa's Missionaries of Charity. Some of us taught English. Some worked in an orphanage. I worked in a streetside clinic near the train station. In the evenings our group would read Luke's gospel together and talk about what we'd seen and done that day.

We lived at the YWCA. It was a lovely old building with long verandas and clay tennis courts that no one seemed to use. We ate our meals there—mostly rice and dal and mangoes and the occasional hard-boiled egg.

I'm not sure how it happened, but we were adopted by several children who lived on the streets. Mostly they were boys, with one or two girls depending on the day. That's how I met Amiroon. One day she just appeared as part of the group.

It's hard to say how old she was. Anywhere from ten to thirteen, I'd guess. Amiroon lived with her mother and two siblings under a bus stop shelter. Malnutrition makes it hard to judge a child's age. We must have asked her how old she was sometime during our stay. Maybe Amiroon was being coy, or maybe she didn't know, but we never did get an answer. So, imagine a ten year old little girl, all knees and elbows and energy.

Amiroon was beautiful. Her hair was tangled and dusty and dark. Her skin was brown. Her eyes were bright and so was her smile. Her feet were bare. Her hands were rough. Her clothes were torn, but she was beautiful.

It seems to me that grace is almost always a surprise. An unexpected gift. Something we don't earn and have no reason to anticipate. C. S. Lewis famously wrote of being surprised by joy. Well, grace has surprised me many times. Most of the time, I'm not even aware of it until later. I'll look back and suddenly there it is. A gift of grace.

But sometimes, and these are the best times, I see grace in the moment it is given. Sometimes I am blessed with eyes to see and ears to hear the truth of what's going on right in front of me. And I feel like a shepherd awakened in the middle of the night by a sky full of angels—awestruck and with a sudden urge to go tell somebody what I've seen.

The children who adopted us were not welcome in the YWCA. So we spent time with them outside on the street. Several of them had come to the city from villages nearby in order to earn money for their families. They were always hungry. Occasionally we'd gather them together and head off to some smoky little restaurant and buy them plates of rice and dal and maybe a little fish. It was the least we could do. And nowhere near enough.

I don't remember Amiroon ever accompanying us to a restaurant. But I do remember the walk she and I took one afternoon.

I was walking to a record store I'd discovered one day while wandering the streets. I wanted to buy an album by Indian classical musician Ustad Ali Akbar Khan. This was near the end of our time in Calcutta. Time for gathering up some tangible pieces of India to help us remember.

For some reason, Amiroon decided to walk with me. I say walk, but you'd do better to imagine something more like a bounce. Amiroon's natural gait was more a hop, skip, and jump than the usual one foot after the other. She laughed and talked and danced all the way to the record store. She waited for me outside. Then she walked me back home again.

On the way, we passed a street vendor selling roasted ears of corn. I asked Amiroon if she wanted an ear to munch on as we walked. She said she did. I paid the vendor and she took the corn and off we went.

Amiroon didn't eat her corn. She just carried it in one hand and danced her way down the street. I wondered why she wasn't eating. "Eat," I said. I wanted her to enjoy the treat. I knew she was hungry. "Eat," I said again.

Amiroon laughed and skipped off down the street. I followed. I kept nagging her to eat the corn—or to tell me why she wouldn't eat it. Finally she took pity on me. She told me why she wasn't eating the corn. She was saving it so she could share it with her family.

A hungry little girl saving an ear of corn so she could share it with her hungry family.

Grace can do many things to us if we see it and pay attention. It can make us laugh or cry. It can break our hearts or strengthen them. It can challenge our faith or nurture it.

The grace is given and for a moment we see the world in a new way. We see it as it was intended to be. As God created it to be. Holy. Just. Generous. Peaceful. Grace-full.

Amiroon. So bright and so beautiful. So poor and so vulnerable. So generous and so kind. A little girl. And a sign of the Christ. The One who came to feed the hungry and to preach good news to the poor.

Our teacher was right. I saw Jesus in Calcutta. And her name was Amiroon.

∽

Ron Adams is the pastor of Madison Mennonite Church in Wisconsin. He is a regular contributor to The Mennonite *and* Rejoice! *magazines. Ron is married to Marilou, and they have two adult sons, Daniel and Benjamin. Their lives were changed forever by discovering Jesus in the streets of Calcutta.*

47

Grace at a Table of Strangers

Heather Derr-Smith

⌒⌒

Smoke hovered in drifts above the heads of the restaurant guests, uncurling in ribbons from glass hookahs. *Sheesha*, a sticky sweet tobacco laced with perfumes of rose, apple, or peach was a Syrian national pasttime. Everywhere you went people were gathered in restaurants and cafes, women nursing babies, families of all generations, young hipsters dressed for clubbing, groups of friends back from evening prayers at the great Umayyad mosque. Charcoal lighters wandered the rooms swinging coals in a burner like an incense boy in the high mass of the Syriac Orthodox church. They pressed the coals to the hookahs and blew at the embers, which glowed their fiery hearts in the dim light.

Outside the city buzzed and hummed with evening hurry. Children waited in line at ice cream shops, tea sellers called out, the glassy windows of the Benetton reflected the street-scene rush of yellow taxis, their back windows plastered with the smiling portrait of Syria's dictator, Bashar al-Asaad. Inside, teenage girls were trying on tight jeans and little black dresses, getting ready for a night of parties and clubs. Damascus in 2007 was a crossroads. Shias from Iran, devout men in beards, and devout women in their black chadors came to Damascus on pilgrimage to the tomb of Sayidda Zeinad, the daughter of the Shia martyr Ali and the granddaughter of the prophet Muhammad. These pilgrims stopped me on the street and asked, "*Amriki?*" and when I answered yes, they grabbed my hands and said joyfully, "*Amriki!* We love you! Our presidents only hate each other, but we love you!"

It was the height of the Iraq war, what the Iraqis in Damascus called the American Occupation. By 2006, a full scale civil war was raging in Baghdad, Samarra, and Fallujah, sending a surge of refugees into neighboring countries. In 2007 there were 1.2 million Iraqi refugees living in Syria. Damascus was a mix of secular, Internet-savvy young activists who were beginning to talk more openly about freedom of expression and government reform, and various religious groups: Catholic Christians, Orthodox Christians, Pentecostals, Wahhabi Muslims in their burkas, Palestinians, and Iraqi Shias and Sunnis. It was a kaleidoscope of cultures and faiths.

I came to Damascus to work on my second book of poems, entitled *The Bride Minaret*. The Bride Minaret, along with the Jesus Minaret, towered above the great Umayyad Mosque. The call to prayer rang out five times a day, calling the faithful to pray. It was post 9/11, in the middle of the War on Terror and I was thinking hard about violence and suffering and God. I decided to go to Damascus to meet ordinary people who had been directly affected by this war.

I was sitting across the table from Fadia, my *fixer*, a guide who facilitates journalists in meeting locals and doing interviews for stories. She was a beautiful young woman in her twenties who spoke perfect English with a British lilt and wore electric green eyeliner. She looked like a young woman you might see at a fashionable club in London. But I had been wary of her for a while. She had called herself an insurgent once, but she sure didn't look like an insurgent, and I didn't understand what she meant. The night before our meeting in the hookah café, a journalist at a dinner party had shown me a video of Fadia that had frightened me. In the video she was dressed quite differently. She wore the Iraqi chador and she told an audience that *any Iraqi who collaborates with the American occupiers should be shot like the traitor they are.* The journalist said he believed she was indeed working with the insurgency in some capacity, but that she also made money as a fixer in Damascus. The insurgency was complicated and there were multiple factions with competing interests. From joyful, hugging Iranians in chadors to fashionable young fixers in green eyeliner, it was sometimes hard to tell the difference between friends and enemies in Damascus.

I had decided to end the relationship with Fadia, but she had called my cell phone with urgency in her voice and said to meet her immediately; she had arranged a meeting with a man who was on his way back into Iraq to ransom his brother being held hostage by the Shia militia. This was a very common occurrence at the time, and refugee families would often have to spend their life's savings to free loved ones back home.

Aabdul came into the café looking frightened. He spoke with Fadia in Arabic and I heard her say, "*Alhamdulillah, Alhamdulillah,*" which literally means "Praise to God" but is also used more colloquially to say, "It's okay." Farida reassured him: "It's okay. She's not a journalist; she's a poet." This seemed to calm him. He sat down with us, and the waiter brought us tea.

Aabdul had survived the worst of the occupation and insurgency. He had witnessed so much violence in Iraq. He saw two young girls shot in a pharmacy right before his eyes, blood and glass everywhere. He watched from the window of his home as a man was executed on a nearby street corner. Things began to grow more and more dangerous for him and his family. They belonged to a small sect called the Sabian Mandaen, targeted as heretics by Islamists. He was eventually kidnapped and tortured and then inexplicably let go.

Sabian Mandaens are an ancient gnostic sect. The word *Sabian* means "baptized" and *Mandean* means "knowledge." They are monotheists who revere Adam, Noah, and John the Baptist and are also pacifists. Their mythology revolves around light and water. I was amazed that this man before me belonged to this small sect and that, in the midst of so much violence and terror, we shared a common commitment to nonviolence. I explained to him that I was Anabaptist, a Mennonite, and that we were also pacifists. We both sat looking stunned at one another.

We spent more than an hour there in that busy café, a Mandaen, a Mennonite, and an insurgent. We talked about baptism and the similarities between our faiths. And then it was time for him to go. He was on his way into a war-ravaged country where his brother's life hung in the balance. We were silent for a few minutes, and then he asked if we would pray for him. Fadia looked taken aback, but I felt the presence of God there with us and I said yes, absolutely. We were three strangers, really, in every sense of the word. Mandaens are not Christians. And I was afraid of Fadia and those with whom she was connected. In some ways we could imagine ourselves as friends; Aabdul and I shared many of the same faith stories of John the Baptist. Yet, in other ways we could have been enemies. I was American and my country was at war with their country. Nevertheless, I felt God's powerful presence there crossing every boundary and working across every border to have a place at the table. We prayed quietly in that busy, smoke-filled café. When we lifted our heads, Aabdul said, "*Alhamdulilla, Alhamdulilla*" (Praise to God).

☾☾

Heather Derr-Smith is a graduate of the Iowa Writers'
Workshop and a poet with two books on themes of war,
suffering, and the presence of God in our broken world.
Her first book, Each End of the World, *is about the war*
in Bosnia in the 1990s. In 2010 she was a visiting poet
at the International University of Sarajevo, the Sarajevo
Gymnasium, and American University in Tulzla where she
led workshops with students who lived through the war.
In 2007 she traveled to Damascus, Syria, to interview
Palestinian and Iraqi refugees for her second book, The
Bride Minaret *(University of Akron Press, 2008). Derr-*
Smith is visiting faculty in Iowa State University's Creative
Writing and the Environment MFA program. She lives in
Des Moines with her husband and three children and is a
member of Des Moines Mennonite Church.

48

Aging with Purpose

Elsie Rempel

∽

I turned sixty the summer of 2012. No big deal you might say. But I was thrilled that I could turn sixty and wasn't dead yet, and even hosted a big "I'm so glad I'm not dead yet party." You see, it could very easily have been otherwise. My life was spared in a head-on collision on a winding two-lane road near Choma, Zambia, in February of that same year. I was on a service leave as a mentor to Zambian teachers through Mennonite Central Committee's Global Family Program. In the process, I learned a lot, developed a lot of respect for the Brethren in Christ educators in Zambia's Southern Province, and offered some practical and pastoral assistance as they struggled to develop better literacy in their students and improve their own morale in a challenging and underappreciated profession.

On the way to my first large, regional workshop, I was involved in a head-on collision, in which the lives of all six who were involved, thanks be to God, were spared. I came out of that experience convinced that God spared my life because my earthly work was not yet done and incredibly grateful for another chance to get old. In addition to bruising and chest compression, I had three breaks in my left ankle, a deep gash and tendon damage to my right ankle, and a major hematoma on my right knee. But I was alive and healing, and so were the others.

On the day after the accident, I was waiting in the hospital courtyard to have my ankles x-rayed. Unbeknownst to me, I was sitting next to two women who were affected by the accident. One was a young woman who had been in the oncoming van. Her stiffly held neck indicated she was suffering from whiplash. The other was the mother of the girl who had also been in the van. She approached us and introduced herself and the other woman. Coincidence or God's grace? I was so glad to see them, to say I was praying for them, to say "sorry, sorry" as they do in Zambia, and to inquire about their health. They said the other driver was well enough to be filing the police report at the moment, and that the girl was already back at school. They gave me a good but sympathetic once-over, and then the woman with whiplash got up and walked slowly away. I hoped my response to them would help their healing. It certainly helped me, though it left me emotionally drained.

My local host and advocate, Eugene, picked up on my exhaustion and called a nearby Zambian friend to come by to pray for me. Pastor Sikala and Martha showed up just after I managed to crawl and hoist myself into the van. They pastored a local African indigenous church. This relatively untrained pastor and his wife proceeded to ask the right questions, exude the right kind of sympathy, and then pray for healing at all the different levels I was hurting. A trained trauma counselor couldn't have done better. I was deeply touched and impressed by them. Another touch of grace.

After two days in a clinic, I spent the next week receiving great care in the Brethren in Christ guest house, just ten meters away from my living quarters. Many Zambian visitors, from the education secretary to the local cleaning lady, came by. They ended each visit by holding my hands in theirs and offering lovely, spontaneous prayers for my healing. Soon, numerous notes from home confirmed that I was being carried on a huge wave of prayer on both sides of the Atlantic. More grace.

On the third night I received a special gift. I woke up around two o'clock in the morning to searing pain, like that of many hot needles poking my ankles. And then the pain was moderated by the strong sensation that my father, who had passed on some years ago, was holding and stroking my ankles with his strong and gentle "bonesetter" hands, smiling at me, and saying in low German, "Well Elstje, what have you done now?" The gift of his healing presence, when the rest of my family was so far away, was incredible. Grace upon grace.

Two weeks after the accident, I led the first of many regional workshops, which I would conduct over the next two months from a wheelchair. In those weeks I had developed a deep appreciation for the Zambians' support. They in turn were deeply moved by my willingness to stay and serve even though I was injured. They were convinced that God had spared my life for a purpose, and part of that purpose was to lead these workshops, so they listened well to this woman who had been saved from the grave.

The meditation I shared at my first set of workshops came from Isaiah's third servant song (Isa 50:4-8a), words that had served as a personal confirmation of the call to go. They continued to speak to me in a variety of ways on my journey of healing. The words also spoke to participants and helped them recognize teaching as a noble, God-given ministry. The teachers learned to realize God had also given them the tongue of a teacher, with a word to sustain the weary. God would open their ears to listen as one being taught and give them the courage to set their faces like flint, to be redeemed from disgrace and vindicated for their efforts at raising up a generation of readers in a setting that could so easily overwhelm.

All too soon it was time to say farewell and return to life and ministry in North America. I did so, filled with gratitude for being well received and having accomplished the ministry I had come for. My return to North America coincided with learning to walk again. In that process, pain continued to teach me how hard to push myself as I regained bone density, flexibility, and muscle strength. Gratitude for a new chance at life, at the chance to grow old, also continued to teach me. It encourages me to live patiently with that other teacher—pain—to love getting older, and to embrace the opportunities for service that God continues to send my way.

And I'm so happy to be sixty.

∞

Elsie Rempel is faith formation consultant for Mennonite Church Canada and a devoted grandmother of four children ages one to twelve. A trained teacher with many years of experience in Christian school classrooms, Elsie devoted much of the last decade to Mennonite Church Canada faith formation ministries. Elsie has written vacation Bible school materials and served as a mentor to elementary school teachers in Zambia's Southern Province through a Mennonite Central Committee program. Currently she seeks to encourage and mentor church lay leaders of all ages through her ministry. Elsie and her husband, Peter, belong to Charleswood Mennonite Church in Winnipeg, Manitoba. They have three married adult children who live nearby.

49

Touched by Grace

Elizabeth Raid

∞

Acup of hot chocolate and a fireside chat with myself seemed the appropriate way to spend the last hours of the year. Endings and beginnings often cause me to wonder and ponder: Where have I been this past year? Where am I headed? Of course, it's fun to review one's physical comings and goings—trips to visit family at a distance, work-related travels, road trips with my husband that offer the opportunity for extended conversations.

But the end-of-year review demands more than the trivial or temporal. What is the state of my soul? How has my spiritual life changed these past months? What have I learned about myself and about others? Has my relationship with Jesus remained stagnant or deepened?

Questions of this significance call for another log on the fire and a second cup of hot chocolate! Rereading my journal from the year's beginning revealed what I feared. I still felt stuck in my life. A troubled close relationship had not improved. In fact, it had worsened in the past months. No new doors for employment options had been opened. Instead, I'd experienced a pay cut due to financial difficulties in the organization. Aging parents had done only that—aged and required more hospital stays and caregiving. When I looked beyond my own little personal situation, the picture only became grimmer and darker. National tragedies, worldwide calamities, and raging wars engaged much of the news and affected millions of lives. The political and economic scenes echoed the same drama and uncertainty. Out-of-control access to guns that became weapons of mass destruction invaded the safety and sanctity of churches, schools, and homes—killing children, youth, adults, and the elderly. Violence and fear became bedfellows in the constant struggle to control and overpower the other.

My despairing thoughts consumed my energy as I drained my second cup of hot chocolate. If I continued down this path, I could easily be sucked into the ways of this world: greed, power, control, fear, violence—the vicious cycle that has ruled our world for centuries. In my own life, I often expressed anxiety over the ongoing drought that threatened to destroy the beauty of the trees and plants surrounding our home and seemed to sap my spirit as well. I felt concern over sufficient financial resources to sustain us as retirement approached. I wished I could make things better not only in my own family, but also for those less fortunate who struggle with daily, life-threatening challenges. My journal entries for my weekly gifts of grace list had ended abruptly several months ago.

During the recent season of Advent, I'd often heard and repeated the words: "Come, Lord Jesus, quickly come." I knew that Jesus was the answer given as God's gift of grace to this broken, yearning world of ours. I just wanted to feel that gift manifest in my life as well as know it with my mind.

I lit the Christ-child candle, still sitting on our table, even here at the end of the year. As I watched its gentle flickering yet constant light, I began to breathe more slowly. The earthy scent of the pine branches on the lit Christmas tree, waiting its final hours before becoming a branch that would be tossed out and blown in the wind, began to ground me in the goodness of God.

I remembered the sweet voices of my six- and nine-year-old grandsons who last evening sat on the piano bench with me and sang "Silent Night, Holy Night" and "Joy to the World." My husband had surprised me by setting the table for our company and washing the dishes and cleaning up afterward. My heart warmed with love for this caring, kind man in my life.

My daughter in a distant state had called to thank us for the gifts and the many ways I'd helped them this past year. She wished us a happy New Year. In a new way I felt the nearness of that parent-child bond that even age cannot sever.

The aging parent had returned from the hospital to the care facility in time to be surrounded with loving family members for Christmas. A period of calm came before the next health crisis.

Over the past year, my intentionality for more silent space had been realized through monthly group spiritual direction. Spending time with like-minded souls who also yearn for a deeper relationship with Christ encouraged me in my own spiritual journey.

I recalled a Christmas morning dream where the troubled relationship with a family member was healed. There were hugs, smiles, and laughter passed around. With that reassuring dream and the other moments when I realized how grace touched my life, I felt the Christ Child born again in my heart.

These soothing sights, sounds, and memories calmed my restless spirit. I closed my eyes and simply breathed *Jesus. Love. Jesus. Love.* As I settled into the silence, Jesus' very presence fanned the fires of God's love, filling my mind and my body with peace. In the new year, I will still need to learn to listen longer and more deeply and to allow space in the silence for God to grow in my heart.

The troubled relationship has not changed in a physical sense. But now I am more content to know God is still working in that person's life, because I know that as far as is humanly possible I have kept love flowing toward that person and lines of communication open. The storms of life on this earth will still rage. God has promised that in the end all things will be well. So because all things are not yet well, I know it is not the end. God is still at work in my life!

∽

Elizabeth Raid lives in Newton, Kansas, with husband, Lou Gomez Jr. They have five children and thirteen grandchildren. Originally from Bluffton, Ohio, she graduated from college there, later receiving her MDiv from Quaker seminary Earlham School of Religion, Richmond, Indiana. She worked for Mennonite Central Committee and currently works part time for another Mennonite institution. She participates in Bethel College Mennonite Church when she is not assisting in her husband's pastorate. Elizabeth writes for various Mennonite publications and recently released her first book: Howard Raid: Man of Faith and Vision, *published by Pandora Press as part of the Mennonite Reflection Series.*

50

Grace for Even Me

Sarah Bixler

∞

It was the first day of spring. Bright yellow petals blinked on my giant daffodils as the sun chased the cold chill from the air. Robins flittered around the yard, playing tag and pecking the soft ground for plump worms and bugs. Signs of new life appeared everywhere. I should have been outside relaxing on the porch swing, enjoying the beautiful day, but I was in the dark, damp basement.

Sitting on the hard concrete floor, doubled over as far as my six-months-pregnant belly would allow, I scrubbed brown water marks from the vinyl tile. Two months earlier a pipe had burst in the nearby wall, the disastrous combination of a hard freeze and a garden hose left hooked up to the outside faucet. Gallons of water had come gushing down the basement walls and spread across the first floor, pouring from the ceiling tiles into the basement and bubbling up between the hardwood planks on the floor above. Washing the basement floor was one of the final clean-up tasks, after drying out and removing damaged boards and patching drywall, and before repainting walls and replacing half of the first floor. And my husband and I were doing the majority of the work.

Long before the entire floor was cleaned, my back hurt and my abdomen protested being folded in half with a baby blocking the way. I hauled my aching body up two flights of stairs and called to my husband that I was taking a nap. It didn't take me long to fall asleep.

When I awoke, the aching feeling persisted. Not in my back anymore, but in my sides and my belly. I tried to find a comfortable position, but there was no relief. I went downstairs where Ben was preparing supper and tried to smile as our two-year-old, Calvin, pedaled around the exposed plywood kitchen floor on his tricycle.

I knew something was wrong. Ben encouraged me to call the doctor, so I placed a message at the hospital for the obstetrician on duty. But after an hour passed, I recognized that I had contractions occurring every five minutes. We drove to the hospital as the last rays of daylight faded from the spring sky.

The next hours became a blur of excruciating contractions, epidural needle, lower abdominal incision, "Do you have a name picked out?" and a glimpse of a small red mass who was our daughter. For three hours we waited for the report that she was still alive and her breathing had stabilized. We briefly touched a tiny hand, barely visible under a quilted aluminum blanket and tubes coming out every which way, before she was rushed to the neonatal intensive care unit (NICU) an hour away.

The doctors described Susannah Rose as feisty and strong at thirteen weeks premature. But within two days, a sudden hemorrhage in her heart sent her fragile systems awry. That first week of spring, we looked at her through tearful eyes and prayed that the bleeding in her heart and brain would stop. Calvin met his little sister at five days old and clasped his small fingers around her hand. And on the seventh day, Ben and I held her in our arms for the first and last time. Shock, pain, and grief hung like a pale haze over the beginning of a season meant to be joyous and full of life.

But despite the loss in my life, spring continued to bloom around me. And gradually my heart opened with the daffodils to God's healing and grace. The first step in this blossoming was making peace with God. I wrestled with why God hadn't intervened. I felt like God had let me down in allowing my daughter to suffer. Had God really begun creating her only to stop halfway through? As I struggled with these faith questions that emerged from the dark, hurt places in my heart, God's Spirit whispered words of peace and comfort. "I cried that first week of spring," God told me, "and I am still weeping with you over the suffering of our beautiful child." And that allowed me to offer grace to a God whom I did not fully understand.

Even easier than extending grace to God was offering grace to others who, along the way, had hurt me unintentionally. I offered grace to the doctor who didn't return my call. To the entry nurse who wasted twenty precious minutes trying to determine whether I was really having contractions. To the birthplace nurse who cheerfully asked me if I wanted my baby in the room with me, a baby struggling for her life an hour away. To the NICU nurse who coolly snapped photos of Susannah after she pulled out her own breathing tube and gasped for air. To Susannah's doctor who reduced her blood pressure medication, resulting in her heart hemorrhaging. To my elderly neighbor who brought a meal and said, "It was for the best. She might have been, you know, bad." To a friend who complimented me on my post-pregnancy figure when all I wanted was to still be pregnant.

I had grace for everyone except myself. I could not shake the thought that I could have prevented Susannah from dying, that I was ultimately responsible for her fate. I could barely look at my shrinking figure in the mirror, a bright red scar in place of where Susannah still should have been growing. I focused my attention instead on the daffodils, tulips, and hyacinths that bloomed in my flowerbeds. They were weeded, mulched, and blooming vigorously long before my doctor had cleared me to begin postsurgery activity. And as my hands plunged deep into the warm soil, God's Spirit taught me that Susannah, like a spring bulb, had blossomed briefly, died, but now knows life where she blooms eternal.

The passage of time and summer's arrival helped me gain a new perspective on Susannah's brief life. Slowly I came to accept that although I may have been able to prevent her early birth, I was still a mother to Susannah. The grief in my heart turned to gratitude for the few moments we spent together. And the longing for what could have been different deepened my love for the precious girl who will always be mine.

I discovered that there is grace for even me.

∞

Sarah Ann Bixler lives in Harrisonburg, Virginia, with her husband, Benjamin, and two children. She received a degree in English education from Eastern Mennonite University and enjoys creative writing. Sarah has worked as a youth minister, teacher, curriculum writer, and administrator in Mennonite churches and institutions throughout her career. Currently, she works for Virginia Mennonite Conference and on Eastern Mennonite University's residence life staff. Sarah will soon be enrolled at Princeton Theological Seminary studying for her master's of divinity degree.

To use this book
in a discussion

Here are some questions that could be asked after reading a group of stories, or individual stories. You will also likely think of your own discussion questions without too much difficulty:

1. What stands out to you from this story (or group of stories)?
2. Have you, or someone you know, had a similar experience? Share.
3. What connected with your heart?
4. What connected with your head and mind?
5. Where would you argue with the writer of the story? Where do you agree?
6. What do you hope you'll remember tomorrow about this story?
7. How can you make changes in your life in light of this story?